Mesopotamian Goddesses

Unveiling Your Feminine Power

WEAM NAMOU

BOOKS BY WEAM NAMOU

The Feminine Art

The Mismatched Braid

The Flavor of Cultures

I Am a Mute Iraqi with a Voice

The Great American Family: A Story of Political Disenchantment

Iraqi Americans: The War Generation

Iraqi Americans: Witnessing a Genocide

Iraqi Americans: The Lives of the Artists

Healing Wisdom for a Wounded World
My Life-Changing Journey Through a Shamanic School
(Book 1)

Healing Wisdom for a Wounded World
My Life-Changing Journey Through a Shamanic School
(Book 2)

Healing Wisdom for a Wounded World
My Life-Changing Journey Through a Shamanic School
(Book 3)

Healing Wisdom for a Wounded World
My Life-Changing Journey Through a Shamanic School (Book 4)

HERMiZ
PUBLiSHING

Copyright © 2019 by Weam Namou

All rights reserved. No part of this book may be reproduced or transmitted in any form or by any means, electronic or mechanical, including photocopying, recording or by any information storage and retrieval system, without permission from the author.

Library of Congress Cataloging-in-Publication Data
2 0 1 8 9 1 4 6 0 8

Namou, Weam
ISBN 9781945371806

Mesopotamian Goddesses
Unveiling Your Feminine Power
(nonfiction)

First Edition

Published in the United States of America by:
Hermiz Publishing, Inc.
Sterling Heights, MI

10 9 8 7 6 5 4 3 2 1

This book is dedicated to my mother, my father, and my heritage.

Contents

Books by Weam Namou iii

Introduction ix

Chapter 1: The Cradle of Civilization 1

Chapter 2: Tiamat, Goddess of the Salt Sea 11

Chapter 3: Ninhursag, Lady of the Mountains 20

Chapter 4: Ningal, The Great Lady 34

Chapter 5: Inanna and Ereshkigal, Goddess of Heaven and Earth, Goddess of the Underworld 47

Chapter 6: Ishtar, Goddess of Fertility, Love, War, and Sex 82

Chapter 7: Ninlil, Lady of the Wind 103

Chapter 8: Enheduanna, Ornament of Heaven 113

Chapter 9: Ninkasi, Goddess of Beer 131

Chapter 10: Gula, The Great Healer 139

Chapter 11: Nanshe, Goddess of Social Justice 147

Chapter 12: Semiramis, Gift of the Sea 155

Chapter 13: Asherah, The Mother Goddess 182

Chapter 14: Lilith and Eve, The First Women 204

Chapter 15: Kubaba, The only queen on the Sumerian King List 215

Chapter 16: Al-Lat, Al-Uzza and Manat, The Three Trinity 222

Chapter 17: Other Deities 231

Chapter 18: Mother of God 237

Notes 243

Notes for the Images 260

Introduction

When I was a child, one of my older sisters, who is eleven years my senior, asked if I wished I had been born a boy. I said no, that I liked being a girl. I didn't at all feel inferior to boys. Only years later, into my adulthood, did I understand why she had asked that question. My youth and innocence had blocked me from seeing the limitations that society often placed on girls and women, and although I didn't know it then, I carried an inner power that stemmed from long, long ago.

I grew up not knowing about the historical and legendary women from my birth country, Iraq, otherwise known as ancient Mesopotamia. Their presence was so obscured by the hostile political and religious environment of the Middle East that I never thought they existed. Luckily, my parents decided to immigrate to the United States where, at the age of ten, inspiration to pursue my dreams began because of the Western women who had created great works of literature, music, medicine, and other accomplishments. As I grew older, I began to learn about my own ancestors.

Maria, my great grandmother, was a legend in her time. She was a powerful businesswoman and a healer. Maria courageously rode horses through the deserts in the northern part of Iraq when it was rare for women to do so. She was so loved and respected in the community that one of her sons abandoned his last name from his father and took on her first name, Maria, as the family surname. His decision caused a separation within the family, given that in a patriarchal society it is customary to take on the paternal name. But I imagine, for him, it was like choosing to say he was Prince Phillip's son when his mother was Queen Elizabeth II.

My paternal Aunt Hassina was a midwife and nurse in Fallujah—a city which dates back to Babylonian times, was host to important Jewish academies for many centuries, and later became known as the city of mosques because of its over 200 mosques. She was one of few Christians in that city, if not the only Christian. She lived there alone with her son after her husband went missing in some war. Mostly she delivered the babies of the wives and daughters of sheiks.

My aunt worked for decades amongst tribes who highly loved and respected her. She also helped save many lives, especially the lives of newborn girls. Long ago, when Fallujah was just a small town, it was customary amongst Arab tribes for the father, if he so desired, to bury a newborn girl. Some men wanted to do just that, and my aunt was such an educated, smart, and compassionate woman that, through words and by citing the Koran, she, a Christian woman, was able to convince them not to.

In my adulthood, I began to discover some of the legendary women of ancient Mesopotamia who had been buried until about a hundred years ago, when archaeologists dug them up and an untold story arose. Thanks to these findings and to the writers, historians, and lecturers who valued the women of that region and therefore kept them alive, there's now plenty of information to read about them. Yet, despite the wealth of material available, the role legendary women played in ancient Mesopotamian history and culture is still a fairly new topic that the majority of people are unaware of. After all, these women's stories were buried for thousands of years and only began to resurface about a hundred years ago.

While ancient Mesopotamia has come to near ruin, the goddesses' original roles as oracles, astrologers, and politicians can still be ascertained from their depictions on stone tablets and pottery art that was collected from archaeological research. Over the years, I found descriptions about them scattered in various books and articles, reminding me of the diaspora of Iraqis. I wanted to place this information under one roof, i.e. book, to recount their tales as a storyteller, not as a historian or academic, and as a woman from their lineage.

Not all the names of the mother goddesses are mentioned within this book, just the prominent ones. Most goddesses had a long list of names because each culture and nation changed her name to suit their language. Many different names overlap and assimilate with other goddess's names or share similar attributes with a particular goddess. For instance, Inanna, the goddess of the Sumerians, is called Ishtar in Akkadian, another Mesopotamian language. The Ishtar iteration of spelling came after Inanna, and Ishtar was the goddess of the Babylonians and Assyrians who inherited much of the Sumerian culture, but their language was different. Both Inanna and Ishtar bear the Queen of Heaven title.

Since the stories were told by people from a civilization with a rich oral tradition, a certain amount of embellishment snuck into these ancient stories, and the embellishments seemed to grow larger from one telling to the next. So it's natural to assume that the stories of these legendary women, similar to all historical accounts that are thousands of years old, are probably a combination of fact and fable.

More importantly, their stories teach us a great deal and are much needed today, given that these women's deliberate removal from the history of that region has caused the Middle East to be in utter shambles. Once a friend, Feather Redfox, wrote to me, "The loss of Mesopotamia's culture is unfathomable to me as is the loss of the feminine power, especially in all the world. It is good for you to be that voice, for I believe the world's only real hope is healing through the feminine."

There was a design and rhythm to the Garden of Eden, a balance and harmony. Then women lost their power through a pattern of falsehoods. We live in a time when people are searching for a new and more balanced way of life. To create that balance, we first must heal the earth by unveiling these stories and putting them back onto the page and into our collective memory. We have to bring forth a transformed understanding of feminine consciousness and create a healthy marriage in society that's based on equal male and female energies.

In the following pages, you'll find divine role models and lessons from thousands of years ago that continue to permeate our culture, their ancient ideas reminding us of the divinity in every human and the goddess in every woman.

Chapter 1

The Cradle of Civilization

Ancient Mesopotamia

The land of milk and honey, known as ancient Mesopotamia and the cradle of civilization, is located between two rivers: the Tigris and the Euphrates. Mesopotamia is mostly modern-day Iraq and Kuwait and parts of Iran, Syria, and Turkey. It is the setting for much of the Old Testament, including the Garden of Eden, the birth of Adam and Eve, and Prophet Abraham.

Some of the most significant developments or inventions credited to the Mesopotamians include writing, the wheel, agriculture, beer, sailboats, irrigation, religious rites, and separation of time into hours, minutes, and seconds (the clock). Many firsts were discovered there: laws, contracts, written music, doctors, bicameral congress, mitigation, mathematics, astronomy, and much more.

Assyriologist George Smith wrote, "The fragments of the Chaldean historian and priest, Berosus, preserved in the works of various later writers, have shown that the Babylonians were acquainted with traditions referring to the Creation, the period before the Flood, the Deluge, and other matters forming parts of Genesis."

A great number of stories come from that region, but up until the last hundred years or so, it seemed as if the men had single-handedly built the civilization that influenced the city-states as we know it today. What role did women play in the building of this great empire that gifted us with our modern-day lifestyle?

I discovered the answers to these questions after my niece Sandy called one day and asked if I'd like to speak about the powerful women of our Chaldean heritage at The Theosophical Society, where she's a board member. As a Chaldean woman, I embraced this topic, not realizing it would become a book.

Before diving into the lives of these women, it's important to become familiar with the history, customs, and people of their birth land. Chaldea was located in the marshy land of the far southeastern corner of Mesopotamia, along the Euphrates and Tigris rivers. In 1927, Leonard Woolley excavated the site and identified it as Ur of the Chaldeas. The chief deity of the city was Nanna, the Sumerian moon-god. Several temples and the great ziggurat were built for him and his consort Ningal, a goddess of reeds in the Sumerian mythology, daughter of Enki and Ninhursag. Ningal and Nanna bore the sun god Utu, his sister Inanna, and Ereshkegal.

The name Chaldean appears to have its origin in the Sumerian title Gal.du, master builder, which later became altered to the pronunciation Kas.du, the singular of Kasdim, through a sound shift well known in the development of the Babylonian language. The Hebrew Bible mentions Ur of the Chaldeas as the birthplace of the Israelite and Ishmaelite patriarch Abraham. According to the table of nations, the biblical Chaldeans descended from Arpachshad, grandson of Noah. Current archaeology work continues to focus on the Ziggurat of Ur, which is located in southern Iraq.

The inhabitants of Chaldea, the Chaldeans, briefly came to rule Babylon, so its people were assimilated into Babylonia. They were the driving force behind the advancement of Babylonian astronomy and science, and their philosophers refined the already established observations and formulated sophisticated theories to describe the cosmological phenomena.

Chaldeans, also known as Neo-Babylonians, speak Aramaic. Their descendants were among the first to embrace Christianity. They are Semites, a name applied to one of the three main divisions of the white race. The two other main white races are the Hamitic and the Japhetic. The term Semitic comes from Shem, the name of one of the sons of Noah, and the classification mentioned above is based on the classification given in the tenth chapter of Genesis. Though the biblical classification is inaccurate, the name Semitic has been retained for convenience. The Semitic group includes the Hebrews (Jews), Assyrians, Chaldeans, Phoenicians, Carthaginians, Arabians, Ethiopians, Babylonians, and various other peoples who share similar physical and intellectual traits.

The three religions which acknowledge one supreme deity—Judaism, Christianity, and Mohammedanism—originated with Semitic races. The Semitic languages are usually divided into northern and southern groups, the former including the ancient dialects of Assyria as well as Babylonia and the Hebrew, Phoenician, and Aramaic tongues. In the Book of Daniel, Chaldean is applied not only to the Babylonian people but to a class of magicians.

Nabopolassar was a central figure in the building of the Chaldean empire. Nebuchadnezzar II, his oldest son and successor, changed the empire by rebuilding the whole city of Babylon. He added a 300-foot ziggurat, double walls, and most importantly, the Hanging Gardens of Babylon. He created the Hanging Gardens as a gift to his Median wife, who was homesick for the plants and gardens of her homeland. In the Hanging Gardens, the plants did not actually hang. They grew from different levels of terraces, like modern-day balconies.

Astronomy and astrology are likely what Chaldea is most known for today. Astronomy was essentially their religion. They built ziggurats, huge structures that acted as temples and that sometimes reached the height of 150 feet. They believed ziggurats were closer to the sky and heaven, and their interest in the ziggurats led to an interest in studying the stars. A big focus for building ziggurats was to bring astrology to Chaldea. The building was the religious center and was a sense of pride for the community. Because of this, the first astronomers were priests.

Early mathematicians in Chaldea came up with the system of dividing the time of sunrise to sunrise into twelve equal parts. They created the sixty-minute system (i.e. 1 hour = 60 minutes) over 3,000 years ago and the time system of day, month, year as well as the Lunar and Solar Calendars. They reached the conclusions that the earth, moon, and another five planets and our sun are all part of one system, a fact that took the world two thousand years to agree with.

Russian noblewoman Helen Petrovna Blavatsky writes, "The ancients were always distinguished—especially the Chaldean astrologers and Magians—for their ardent love and pursuit of knowledge in every branch of science. They tried to penetrate the secrets of nature in the same way as our modern naturalists, and by the only method by which this object can be obtained, namely: by experimental researches and reason. If our modern philosophers cannot apprehend the fact that they penetrated deeper than themselves into the mysteries of the universe, this does not constitute a valid reason why the credit of possessing this knowledge should be denied them or the imputation of superstition laid at their door. Nothing warrants the charge; and every new archaeological discovery militates against the assumption. As chemists they were unequalled."

Ancient Mesopotamians' great achievements in many scientific fields still impact us and are being used today, but for a long time, and in many cases even now, the women who helped build this civilization are silenced by historians.

Goddess

A goddess is a female deity; a woman of great beauty or grace; a woman adored as a deity. Webster describes deity as one exalted or revered as extremely good or powerful. The goddess movement includes spiritual beliefs and practices which emerged predominantly in North America, Western Europe, Australia, and New Zealand in the 1970s. The movement grew as a reaction to perceptions of predominantly male-dominated organized religion and consists of goddess worship and a focus on gender and femininity.

The Bible says, in the very first chapter of Genesis, that man and woman were created in the image of God. Spirit has no gender. Gender is a human attribute and God is a mystery, personally visualized by each person and beyond any physical description, neither human nor sexual in nature, and yet scripture describes God with physical characteristics such as arms and feet and non-physical attributes such as anger, jealousy, and repentance. It also refers to God as He and a Father even though God is not a man.

About a hundred years ago, the existence of the goddess began to emerge when archaeologists found magnificent discoveries that revolutionized peoples' understanding of religion. Small female figures and other artifacts surfaced that proved ten thousand years before Christ, women invented complex tools used for agriculture, ceramics, medicine, textiles, and the written language. The goddess was not merely a fertility cult object; she was a deity, a symbol of female mystery. The religious ideas of early humans are abundantly documented in their tombs, temples, stone tablets, and painted pottery.

In early Bronze Age Mesopotamia, the cultures that eventually became known as the great kingdoms of Mesopotamia once consisted of peaceful, agriculturally-oriented people. This agricultural civilization relied on the bounties of the earth to provide for them, and they had a very special relationship with the land through the goddess of the earth, the Great Mother.

Eventually, however, there were invasions and an introduction to brutal warfare from Semitic tribes from the north and Aryans to the south. These tribes introduced more patriarchal customs as well as the worship of male sky gods over female earth deities. As the political and military situations in these cultures became more complex and more violent, the societal position of women, unfortunately, decreased. Prior to this, women enjoyed a prominent place in the public life of ancient Mesopotamians.

Under the reign of King Hammurabi of Babylon (1792-1750 BCE), goddesses were increasingly replaced by gods. During this patriarchal revolution, the great goddesses were expelled from this male-defined ideology and the sky god was elevated to a monotheistic status, marking all other deities as false idols, undeserving of worship. This is partly why we don't know more about this portion of our history.

Dr. Bettany Hughes notes that if we look at the figurines made between about 40,000 BC until around 5,000 BC—a period which sees the flourishing of the modern mind—we'd notice that at that time around 90 percent of all these figurines are of women. So women, she says, are very present in the archaeological record but then start to disappear once pre-history turns into history.

According to researcher and author Merlin Stone, the goddess religion did not fade away. It was ruthlessly destroyed over time by conquering northern tribes. Evidently the annihilation of Her peaceful and prosperous culture was so violent that that region has since been in constant war. Without Her, the land once known for milk and honey and the Garden of Eden has turned into a hell on earth, especially for women.

Religion

The Sumerians were devout people. In most statues, you see their hands at their hearts. They didn't take ownership of their creations and developments and instead considered what they created as gifts from the gods. Hammurabi wrote the first law but claimed it was given to him by the god Shamash. For them, the way they expressed devotion to God was by working for God.

Polytheism was practiced by the inhabitants of ancient Mesopotamia, but the Sumerians believed in four main gods of heaven, air, earth, and water with one reigning supreme.

Chaldeans are said to have believed in one impersonal, universal deific principle, although they never mentioned It, and offered worship to the solar, lunar, and planetary gods and rulers, regarding the stars and other celestial bodies as their respective symbols.

According to H.P. Blavatsky, Noah, or Nuah, like all the euhemerized manifestations of the unrevealed one, was androgynous. In some instances, he belonged to the very feminine triad of the Chaldeans, known as Nuah, the universal Mother. Every male triad had its feminine counterpart. Merlin writes that people revered their supreme creator as female, that the Great Goddess, the Divine Ancestress, had been worshiped from the beginnings of the Neolithic periods of 7000 BC until the closing of the last goddess temples, around AD 500.

Patricia Monaghan wrote that the empires of Mesopotamia extended into lands now occupied by Palestine, Israel, Jordan, Lebanon, and Syria. There, Judaism and Christianity were born. In this "Holy Land," archaeology finds evidence of settlement as early as the seventh millennium BCE. But whereas the books of the Jewish Bible describe a religion monotheistic from the start, archaeology unveils a different history.

Digs at Jericho and other sites, often centered upon "tells," or earthen hills above settlements, show a religion involving a primary goddess. Hundreds of images of this primary goddess, sculpted in clay, have been found. This region, the homeland of the Israelite peoples, was also home to the Canaanites, a term that was never clearly defined. Ancient sources use it to refer to non-Israelites. The Hebrew Scriptures describe all goddesses as foreign, or "Canaanite" imports, but archaeological finds suggest that goddesses existed in the earliest Israelite religion. Although evidence for a consort to the high god YHWH has recently become more widely known, conservative Jewish and Christian theologians argue that monotheism was a cornerstone of the religions.

First there was a physical destruction of the statues and sanctuaries of the female deities, recorded in the Bible over forty times, such as when Yahweh in Deuteronomy 12:2, 3 commands, "You shall utterly destroy all the places, wherein the nations which ye shall possess served their gods, upon the high mountains, and upon the hills, and under every green tree; and you shall overthrow their altars, and break their pillars, and burn their groves with fire; and you shall hew down the graven images of their gods, and destroy the names of them out of that place."

Then there was the attempt to remove Her from memory.

American surgeon Leonard Shlain wrote that, "In their attempts to solve the mystery of the Goddess's dethronement, various authors have implicated foreign invaders, the invention of private property, the formation of archaic states, the creation of surplus wealth, and the educational disadvantaging of women. While any or all of these influences may have contributed, I propose another; the decline of the Goddess began when some clever Sumerian first pressed a sharp stick into wet clay and invented writing. The relentless spread of the alphabet two thousand years later spelled Her demise. The introduction of the written word, and then the alphabet, into the social intercourse of human initiated a fundamental change in the way newly literate cultures understood their reality. It was this dramatic change in mindset, I propose, that was primarily responsible for fostering patriarchy."

Yet it is through the same measures, writing, that we are bringing Her back to life.

Chapter 2

Tiamat
Goddess of the Salt Sea

Once upon a time in ancient Mesopotamia, there lived a goddess of the sea named Tiamat, also known as Namma (feminine) and Nammu/Namou (masculine), the latter name meaning blessing. She mated with Apsu, the god of fresh sweet water, and their consummation created younger gods who spread over the land to serve various purposes, most notably the building of the cradle of civilization. Like all couples with children running loose, their home became rowdy and chaotic, more intolerable for the husband than the wife.

Apsu detested this change to the point of one day telling his wife, Tiamat, that conceiving the children was a dire mistake and, therefore, the children ought to be destroyed. Of course, she, the mother, was against such a horrid idea. She loved her children dearly, but she couldn't seem to appease and deter her husband from destroying them. Determined to get rid of the children and finally regain peace, Apsu turned to his vizier Mammu for help.

Needless to say, the younger gods were not in favor of being destroyed, so they fought back. They formulated a plan to have Enki, the god of magic and patron of all arts and crafts, cast a spell upon Apsu and Mummu and then kill them both. Enki carried out this plan successfully to the shock and horror of Tiamat, who wanted neither her husband nor her children killed. Outraged, she decides to avenge her husband's murderers by creating an army of chaos to help her.

In the *Enuma Elish*, the Babylonian epic of creation which mostly focuses on the battle between Marduk and Tiamat, Tiamat creates an army of monsters led by her new consort, Kingu. She also tries to establish Kingu as the leader of all the gods by handing him the Tablets of Destiny. In return, the younger gods appoint the storm-god Marduk to destroy Tiamat. Marduk agrees with the condition that, if he destroys Tiamat, he becomes their leader afterward. They accept this offer and he prepares for the battle.

Marduk makes a bow, fletches arrows, grabs a mace, throws lightning before him, fills his body with flame, makes a net to encircle Tiamat with, gathers the four winds so that no part of her could escape, and creates seven horrible new winds such as whirlwinds and tornados. He also creates his mightiest weapon, the rain-flood. Then he sets out for battle, mounting his storm-chariot drawn by four horses, or in some versions of the story riding a dragon. In his lips he holds a spell and in one hand he clasps an herb meant to work against Tiamat's poison.

He arrives to the battle ground and challenges Tiamat, who stands amongst her army, to a single combat. She accepts and advances toward him while shouting spells. He encircles her with the net, blows her up with the winds, and shoots an arrow into her belly, splitting her down the middle. Marduk makes from her ribs the vault of heaven and earth, the Tigris and Euphrates from her weeping eyes, mist from her saliva, mountains from her breasts, and her tail becomes the Milky Way. He defeats the rebel gods and slays Kingu, whose red blood is mixed with red clay of the earth to make the body of mankind, created to act as the servant of the younger Igigis, the gods of heaven.

Marduk takes the Tablets of Destiny, which are fastened to Kingu's breast, making sure it lays on his own breast. There's an ancient image of Marduk where he's clearly seen wearing them. Tablets of Destiny, assumed to be a type of Babylonian Book of Fate since its description and contents aren't available, gave the owner a position of considerable power and importance. After his battle victory, Marduk is given fifty names and honored as king of the gods. The story of *Enuma Elish* ends here.

Tiamat's legend has two parts. In the first, she is a goddess who peacefully designs, through a sacred marriage between salt and fresh water, the cosmos by birthing continuous generations. She epitomizes the beauty of the feminine and is described as the glistening one. In the second part, she is considered the monstrous embodiment of prehistoric chaos, often described as a dragon or sea serpent, wreaking havoc on the younger generation of gods. Some even compare her to the Hebrew entity Leviathan.

In Babylonian religion, the Akitu Festival was dedicated to Marduk's victory over Tiamat to celebrate the taming of primitive chaos. But originally, Akitu marked two festivals celebrating the beginning of each of the two half years of the Sumerian calendar, the sowing of barley in autumn and the cutting of barley in spring.

The Tiamat myth is one of the earliest recorded versions of the Chaoskampf, a German word which means "struggle against chaos," depicting a battle between a cultural hero deity and a chaos monster. Robert Graves considered Tiamat's death by Marduk evidence for his theory that there had been an ancient shift in power from a matriarchal society to a patriarchy.

Grave's ideas were later developed into the great goddess principle by Marija Gimbutas, Merlin Stone, and other writers. The theory suggests Tiamat and other ancient monster characters were presented as former supreme deities of peaceful, woman-centered religions that were turned into monsters when violent. Their defeat at the hands of a male hero corresponded to the manner in which male-dominated religions overthrew ancient society.

"Marduk, the new god of this rather new city, certainly had no right to appropriate to himself the glory of so great a deed ... But in Hammurabi's time Babylon was the center of the kingdom ... Marduk, backed by Hammurabi's armies, could now claim to be the most important god in the land," wrote Professor Edward Chiera.

Jean Shinoda Bolen, M.D., believed that the Great Goddess became the subservient consort of the invaders' gods, and attributes of power that originally belonged to a female deity were expropriated and given to a male deity. Rape appeared in myths for the first time, and myths arose in which the male heroes slew serpents, symbols of the Great Mother. A coiled serpent resting at the base of the human spine is the symbol of Kundalini, latent divine female energy. American comparative religions scholar Joseph Campbell, who went to India as a young man, describes the concept of Kundalini as follows:

> The figure of a coiled female serpent—a serpent goddess not of "gross" but "subtle" substance—which is to be thought of as residing in a torpid, slumbering state in a subtle center, the first of the seven [chakras], near the base of the spine: the aim of the yoga then being to rouse this serpent, lift her head, and bring her up a subtle nerve or channel of the spine to the so-called "thousand-petaled lotus" (Sahasrara) at the crown of the head…She, rising from the lowest to the highest lotus center will pass through and wake the five between, and with each waking, the psychology and personality of the practitioner will be altogether and fundamentally transformed.

The people who killed her husband expected Tiamat to be removed from her emotions. Her rage at this heinous crime was considered so violent and inappropriate that Marduk agreed to destroy her in exchange for gaining lordship over the gods, for the first time in Babylonian history reaching a level of worship close to monotheism. In this way, Tiamat, the female principle who wanted to protect her family, who wanted to stand up for injustice and create a peaceful environment, was silenced. The wound for women was planted.

For thousands of years, there has been a notion that a woman must be silenced, oppressed, and kept in her place to stop her from speaking the truth, especially as it pertains to men. This notion didn't only exist in the Middle East. Almost 3000 years ago in Western culture, Homer's *Odyssey* had a passage that portrayed a similar attitude.

In the story, Penelope, the wife of Odysseus, comes down from her private quarters into the great hall of the palace. She discovers a poet performing to a crowd, singing about the difficulties the Greek heroes are having reaching home. She doesn't particularly like this song and in front of everyone asks him for another, cheerier one. Her young son Telemachus intervenes and says, "Mother, go back up into your quarters and take up your own work, the loom and the distaff... speech will be the business of men, all men, and of me most of all; for mine is the power in this household." So she goes back upstairs.

Author Mary Beard elaborates on this, writing:

> In the early fourth century BC, Aristophanes devoted a whole comedy to the "hilarious" fantasy that women might take over running the state. Part of the joke was that women couldn't speak properly in public—or rather, they couldn't adapt their private speech (which in this case was largely fixated on sex) to the lofty idiom of male politics. In the Roman world, Ovid's Metamorphoses—that extraordinary mythological epic about people changing shape (and probably the most influential work of literature on Western art after the Bible)—repeatedly returns to the idea of the silencing of women in the process of their transformation. Poor Io is turned by the god Jupiter into a cow, so she cannot talk but only moo; while the chatty nymph Echo is punished so that her voice is never her own, merely an instrument for repeating the words of others. In Waterhouse's famous painting she gazes at her desired Narcissus but cannot initiate a conversation with him, while he—the original 'narcissist'—has fallen in love with his own image in the pool.

Although Jesus treated women with respect, not as inferiors, and spoke to them in public about various matters including spirituality, in the Bible women are discouraged from speaking, as noted in Timothy 2:12. "I permit no woman to teach or to have authority over men; she is to keep silent." This cultural view that existed during Jesus' time survived despite His efforts, through demonstration, to give women a voice.

Women leaders today still fear voicing their opinion, as it comes with a price. They might be ostracized, criticized, or rejected, their ideas shrugged off as another feminist complaint or drowned out by male voices or her own critical voice. If they express any anger, they're considered unfeminine and oftentimes given offensive labels. Women tend to be overly emotional as a result of bottling up their words for too long and not knowing how to clearly articulate their needs, feelings, and desires to their loved ones, let alone to the world. When the words finally come out, it may be as an outburst, like bullets shot frantically into the air without an aim or understanding of the bullet.

Many still honor Tiamat and believe that she can be called upon for magical works that deal with harsh truths and confronting chaos before passing on to the next phase of their lives, or the afterworld. She helps us see our darkness, therefore protecting us from gullibility and deceit and allowing us to harmoniously live with others without having to completely subdue our instinctual desires so we can express our whole being.

Psychiatrist Carl Jung suggested we each have a dark side, called "the shadow," which is comprised of all the traits that we want to deny we have. By repressing rather than acknowledging feelings such as anger, jealousy, selfishness, certain sexual desires or needs, we risk projecting the shadow self onto others, causing them harm and suffering. In acknowledging and accepting these traits, you take responsibility for yourself and they stop having control over you.

I studied shamanism for four years, under the apprenticeship of bestselling author and mystic Lynn V. Andrews. Through this ancient teaching, where we learned to choreograph energy, I began to view mental disorder differently, especially in women who, compared to men, are more prone to anxiety, depression, and hysteria—although this is now increasingly affecting both sexes in Western society. People often end up taking pills, deflecting, avoiding their feelings, and trying to control the outcome solely through positive thinking.

The truth is, in the end, prayer, positive thinking, and affirmations are not enough. If we don't deal with our inner condition head on, facing the good and the bad, the opportunity to reconcile our energies within the physical and spiritual world will slip away. Dealing with our inner condition head on will help us not only heal and grow but also bridge a way between Heaven and Earth. Before we go out into the world and speak our truth, whether verbally or nonverbally through creation, we must first speak it within ourselves. This is where silence is golden.

Until you are balanced and know how to remain in your center, where outward situations or harsh words aren't able to easily throw you off track, it's healthy to become invisible for a while, partly by participating in a good dose of silence. Silence allows us the opportunity for self-reflection, to tune in to nature, and it guides us on our own sacred path. Silence protects our thoughts, words, and ideas, and then, after nurturing and replenishing our spirits with a sacred dialogue—through various sacred tools including prayer, meditation, journaling, and communicating with those who've walked similar paths before us—we too will attain a certain state of wisdom that we can verbally share, if we choose to, with the world.

My Native American teacher passed down to his students this simple but profound exercise. The exercise helps you identify your shadow self and heal it, so that when you speak about yourself, there is less anger and more peace, less judgment and more self-worth, less unkindness and more self-love. Make a list of ten things you like about yourself and then make a list of ten things you dislike about yourself. Keep the list for seven days, reading it daily. On the seventh day, create a quiet atmosphere of ceremony—for instance, light candles and burn incense or take a walk in nature. Surrender yourself with an attitude of gratitude. Start a bonfire or fireplace or fill a bowl with water and Clorox. Give thanks for all the attributes that you like and dislike about yourself as you watch the list burn in the fire or dissolve in the water, returning to the universe that gifted you with those attributes to begin with.

Chapter 3

Ninhursag
Lady of the Mountains

One of Tiamat's children was Ninhursag, which means "Lady of the Mountain." The goddess of fertility and the sacred mountains, she was the Great Mother who created both divine and mortal entities and regularly nourished the kings of Sumer with her milk. She was known by over a dozen other names including Nintu, Ki, Gaia, Damkina, Ninlil, depending on her role and which culture and time period was naming her. Ninhursag was the half-sister and wife of Enki, also known as Ea, the god of wisdom, magic, and fresh water.

The Sumerian story *Enki and Ninhursag* compares greatly to the story of the Garden of Eden in the Bible, with texts describing a paradise similar to Eden, only it was called Dilmun. Dilmun, home for the gods on Earth, was created in the winter season. It was a pure and virginal land, clean and bright, where people didn't suffer from disease, headaches, or old age. The land knew peace and didn't need administrators to supervise its people.

Enki and Ninhursag

Pure are the cities—and you are the ones to whom they are allotted. Pure is Dilmun land. Pure is Sumer—and you are the ones to whom it is allotted. Pure is Dilmun land. Pure is Dilmun land. Virginal is Dilmun land. Pristine is Dilmun land.

He laid her down all alone in Dilmun, and the place where Enki lain down with his spouse, that place was still virginal, that place was still pristine. He laid her down all alone in Dilmun, and the place where Enki had lain down with Ninsikila, that place was virginal, that place was pristine.

In Dilmun the raven was not yet cawing, the partridge not cackling. The lion did not slay, the wolf was not carrying off lambs, the dog had not been taught to make kids curl up, and the pig had not learned that grain was to be eaten. When a widow had spread malt on the roof, the birds did not yet eat that malt up there. The pigeon then did not tuck its head under its wing.

No eye-diseases said there, "I am the eye disease." No headache said there, "I am the headache." No old woman belonging to it said there, "I am an old woman." No old man belonging to it said there, "I am an old man." No maiden in her unwashed state resided in the city. No man dredging a river said there, "It is getting dark." No herald made the rounds in his border district. No singer sang an *elulam* there. No wailings were wailed in the city's outskirts there.

It was in Dilmun that Enki met Ninhursag and fell in love. The couple became husband and wife. Yet despite the heavenly state of Dilmun, Ninhursag felt something was missing. Because its soil didn't have fresh water, Dilmun was not yet fruitful. Its fields didn't grow grains and vegetables. So one day, she says to Enki, "This city has no river quay, no fields, nor furrow. What good is it for me?"

He replies, "When Utu the sun god rises into heaven, at that time fresh waters will run from the standing vessels." As a result of Enki's blessing,

> The waters rose up from it into her great basins. Her city drank water aplenty from them. Dilmun drank water aplenty from them. Her pools of salt water indeed became pools of fresh water. Her fields, glebe, and furrows indeed produced grain for her. Her city indeed became an emporium on the quay for the Land. Dilmun indeed became an emporium on the quay for the Land. At that moment, on that day, and under that sun, so it indeed happened.

Enki transforms Dilmun into a divine garden, green with an abundance of harvest. It thrives as the center of commerce and trade and hosts trade ships from Sumer as well as many foreign lands. Life is blessed with resources and happiness. Then, although the story has already announced them husband and wife who lay together in the fields, a more explicit love-making scene transpires.

In the second part of the story, Enki is in the marshes, digging his private part into the dykes and reed beds. He advances toward Ninhursag who nobly pulls his private part aside and cries out, "No man takes me in the marsh." But he strongly desires her, as she is the fertile Mother Earth, and her union with him would ensure the sustenance of life.

In response to her resistance, he says, "By the life's breath of heaven I adjure you! Lie down for me in the marsh, lie down for me in the marsh, that would be joyous!" He then lays down with her, "distributing his semen into her womb," and she conceives a child. Within nine days, she gives birth to a daughter they name Ninsar, Lady of Vegetation. The season begins to change, from winter to spring, causing Ninhursag to depart from Dilmun, the earth which is situated between the heavens and the underworld, so that she can give birth to other parts of the world. She leaves Enki behind to take care of the waters and her daughter Ninsar, who within nine days has grown up to be a beautiful woman.

One day, Ninsar goes to the riverbank where Enki sees her from the marshes. He's attracted to her and says to his minister Isimud, "Is this nice young woman not to be kissed? She's beautiful and so she should be kissed." His minister agrees and, when Enki steps into his boat, Isimud sails the boat upstream to Ninsar. As soon as he steps out of the boat, Enki kisses Ninsar and lays down with her. She conceives a child and on the ninth day, like her mother, she gives birth to a daughter who she names Ninkura, a word that's associated with cultivation.

Ninkura grows up to be a beautiful woman within nine days and one day she goes out to the riverbank. Enki sees her there from the marsh and is attracted to her. He says to his minister, "Is this nice young woman not to be kissed? She is beautiful, and so she should be kissed." His minister agrees and, when Enki steps into his boat, Isimud navigates the boat upstream to Ninkura. As soon as he steps out of the boat, Enki kisses her and lays down with her. She conceives a child, like her mother, and on the ninth day, she gives birth to a daughter who she names Ninimma, which is associated with thirst.

This pattern is repeated with Ninimma, but with her daughter, Uttu, the Exalted Lady, the story changes. This time, Ninhursag intervenes. She says to Uttu, "Let me advise you, and may you take heed of my advice. From in the marsh one man is able to see up here. From in the marsh Enki is able to see up here, is able to see up here, he is. He will set eyes on you."

The text breaks off here for ten lines, so it's unclear what Ninhursag advises her great granddaughter to do next. When the text is legible again, the story continues with Enki arriving at Uttu's door. Apparently following Ninhursag's directions, Uttu tells Enki that she won't sleep with him, or in her own words, allow him to "have hold of my halter," unless he goes to the garden and brings her "cucumbers and apples with their stems sticking out and grapes in their clusters."

He accepts the offer and returns. He knocks on her door, demanding, "Open it! Open it!"

"Who are you?" she asks.

"I'm a gardener. Let me give you cucumbers, apples, and grapes for your 'Yes.'"

Uttu joyfully opens the door and Enki provides her with the fruits and vegetables she requested. He grabs the beer cask and pours for her a generous amount of beer. She waves her hands for him, giving him consent to make love to her. He clasps her to his bosom, lying between her legs, fondles her thighs with his hand, kisses her and makes love to her.

Uttu cries out, "Woe, my thighs! Woe, my liver! Woe, my heart!"

Ninhursag later removes Enki's semen from Uttu's thighs and, with it, grows eight plants: the tree plant, honey plant, vegetable plant, atutu plant, astaltal plant, amharu plant, alfafa grass, and one other illegible plant. When Enki sees the new plants, he's curious about what they are. He asks his minister, "What is this one?" and "What is that one?" To which Isimud, who knew each by name, told him, then plucked each plant and handed it to Enki, who ate each plant. Enki determined the destiny of the plants, had them know it in their hearts to define their role.

Ninhursag is outraged that Enki has eaten all the plants and determined their fates when she's the one who planted them. She curses him, declaring, "Until his dying day, I will never look upon him with life-giving eye." Enki gets sick to the point of dying and the Anunnaki, the gods, helplessly sit down in the dust, distraught at the falling out of Enki and his partner. Ninhursag, the only person who can revive him, has left and they can't find her.

A fox comes to Enlil, leader of the gods, and says, "If I bring Ninhursag to you, what will be my reward?"

"If you bring Ninhursag to me, I shall erect two birch trees for you in my city and you will be renowned."

The fox first anoints his body, shaking out his fur and putting kohl on his eyes. When he finds Ninhursag and tells her of the situation, she hastens to the temple. The Anunnaki slip off her garment and usher the weak Enki to her. She has him sit by her vulva, and looking at him with life-giving eyes, she says to him, "My brother, what part of you hurts you?"

There are eight parts of Enki that hurt him. First, he responds, "The top of my head hurts me." She takes the affliction into her womb and gives birth to Abu out of it. She continues with this questioning, with him giving a different answer each time: "The locks of my hair hurt me." She gives birth to Ninsikila out of it. "My nose hurts me." She gives birth to Ningiritud out of it. "My mouth hurts me." She gives birth to Ninkasi out of it. "My throat hurts me." She gives birth to Nazi out of it. "My arm hurts me." She gives birth to Azimua out of it. "My ribs hurt me." She gives birth to Nin-ti out of it. "My sides hurt me." She gives birth to Enzag out of it.

Thus, Enki was healed and eight healing deities are born—four males and four females—with each of the deities' names related to the part they were born out of and each given a most promising destiny.

Ninhursag healed him by sending her soul into his body.

Historians have noted numerous parallels between myths involving Ninhursag and the Genesis account in the Bible, including the story of Adam and Eve in the Garden of Eden. Ninhursag shapes clay figurines mixed with the flesh and blood of a slain minor deity, who gave himself for the higher good, and ten months later, humans are born. She controls the population growth after the Great Flood, gives birth easily and without pain, but then feels birth pangs after she leaves the marshes and conceives Enki's child on dry land. She curses Enki's lust for sex and his eating of the sacred plants in the Sumerian paradise, heals his diseased body through the rib, and soon gives birth to Nin-ti, or Lady Rib. But in Mesopotamia and Sumer, there was no fall from grace, because humankind was created to be co-workers with the Great Gods in the makings of existence.

Orientalist Samuel Noah Kramer asked, "How does all this compare with the biblical paradise story? First, there is some reason to believe that the very idea of a divine paradise, a garden of the gods, is this Sumerian origin. This Sumerian paradise was located, according to our poem, in the land of Dilmun, a land that was probably situated in southwestern Persia. It is the same Dilmun that, later, the Babylonians, the Semitic people who conquered the Sumerians, located their 'Land of the living,' the home of their immortals. There is good indication that the biblical paradise, which is described as a garden planted eastward in Eden, from whose waters flow four world rivers including the Tigris and Euphrates, may have been originally identical with Dilmun, the Sumerian paradise-land."

Kramer makes several comparisons that include the watering of Dilmun by the sun god to that of the biblical 'but there went up a mist from the earth, and water the whole face of the ground' (Genesis 2:6). That the goddess could give birth without pain or travail illuminates the background of the curse against Eve that it shall be her lot to conceive and bear children in sorrow. And Enki's eating of the eight plants and the curse against him for this misdeed calls to mind when Adam and Eve ate the fruit of the tree of knowledge, and the curse pronounced against each of them for this sinful action. Kramer writes that perhaps the most interesting result of our comparative analysis is the explanation provided by the Sumerian poem for one of the most puzzling motifs in the biblical paradise story—the famous passage describing the fashioning of Eve, 'the mother of all living,' from the rib of Adam.

Why a rib? Why did the Hebrew storyteller find it more fitting to choose a rib rather than any of the other organs of the body for the fashioning of a woman whose name, Eve, according to the biblical notion, means approximately 'She who makes live?' The reason becomes clear if we assume that a Sumerian literary background, such as that represented by the Dilmun poem, underlies the biblical paradise tale.

In this Sumerian poem, one of Enki's sick organs is the rib.

The Sumerian word for 'rib' is ti, pronounced tee. The goddess created for the healing of Enki's rib is called Nin-Ti, 'The lady of the rib.' But the Sumerian word ti also means 'to make live.' The name Nin-Ti may therefore mean 'the lady who makes live' as well as 'the lady of the rib.' It was this, one of the most ancient of literary puns, which was carried over and perpetuated in the biblical paradise story, although here, of course, it loses its validity, since the Hebrew word for 'rib' and that for 'who makes live' have nothing in common.

Ninhursag and Enki are the first divine couple and they conceive all the Great Gods, the Igigi and Anunnaki, the most powerful deities in the pantheon whose primary function is to decree the fates of humanity. They have a passionate relationship with lots of mutual happy teasing and Enki oftentimes considerately succumbs to Ninhursag. Their relationship tells of a time where gender and sex were more balanced. In her writings, Enheduanna, the princess, high priestess and first recorded writer in history, considered Ninhursag the most powerful image of the Divine Feminine.

Joshua J. Mark writes, "In the myth of *Enki and Ninmah (Ninhursag)*, Ninhursag begins on equal footing with the god, but by the end, loses her status. It is known that the female deities in Mesopotamia were overshadowed by the males during the reign of Hammurabi of Babylon (1792-1750 BCE)... Ninhursag experienced this same decline as the other goddesses, and by the time of the fall of the Assyrian Empire in 612 BCE, she was no longer worshiped. Her influence is considered significant, however, in the development of later goddesses as she has been associated with Hathor and Isis of Egypt, Gaia of Greece, and Cybele of Anatolia, the later Magna Mater of Rome."

Ninhursag was a lover, wife, and mother. She also worked outside the home. When the seasons changed, from winter to spring, she departed from Dilmun, her paradise, so she could give birth to and nurture other parts of the world. She left Enki, her consort, behind to take care of the land and her daughter. Evidently, he didn't do such a good job. His lust caused him not to recognize his own daughter when she became an adult. So he pursued her, slept with her, impregnated her, and later repeated the same behavior with her daughter, his granddaughter, and so on down the generations with the women in his family.

Hearing of his uncontrollable sexual conduct, Ninhursag returned to Dilmun to put a stop to it. She planted from his semen eight sacred plants and he took it upon himself to assign the plants' divine destinies when it was her job to do so. He then carelessly ate all the plants, which made Ninhursag so angry, she cursed him. He fell ill and the gods urged Ninhursag to heal him.

Ninhursag, known for her nurturing ways, didn't have the heart to really hurt Enki. Despite his wrongdoing, she comes to his bedside and nurtures and revives him back to good health. Furthermore, from each of his eight ailments, including the rib, she gives birth to eight gods whose godly characteristics serve the world. She turned a bad experience into a good one.

Thousands of years ago, Ninhursag experienced what many women are going through today—balancing the role of a wife, mother, and worker. But Ninhursag's story is absent of gender inequality. She shared her wants and desires with her husband, he listened and abided to her suggestions regarding the addition of water to Dilmun. Without doubts or struggle, she left her home to attend to other business. Her husband didn't try to stop her and he remained at home to watch the land and their daughter. When she returned, she didn't blame his gender for his harmful behavior, but she also didn't take a back seat. She confidently pushed back and pushed forward, trusting her instincts and making decisions quickly, choosing not to look away from an important matter. She used her wisdom and strength to turn a bad situation to a good situation. She brought peace back to Dilmun without having to hurt anyone.

We are all encouraged to go for what we want in our careers, to never give up, but for women, the path is different. Women face challenges that many of their male counterparts don't understand because historically they haven't had to deal with these issues. Achieving high positions isn't an easy task for women and once they do achieve it, they oftentimes get paid less for it. Some mothers have to choose between staying home to raise their children or pursuing a career. Those who work outside the house end up doing a second shift of housework and childcare when they return home from work, with an expectation to be ideal mothers. These expectations cause many women to have to choose between having a family or a career. Luckily, in many instances, technology's evolution allows modern women to be stay-at-home moms and hold a career.

To reclaim our feminine power, we can help nudge the world closer to gender equality and fairness so that women don't have lower wages and men take more responsibility for the children and stop using violence. One way is by adopting ideas from countries that have done a relatively good job of narrowing the gender gap. For example, Netherland's emancipation policy of 1978 ensured that parental leave, care, income, power, decision, education, and salaries remained equal between men and women. The government provides benefits to new mothers, including giving them access to a maternity nurse with part or all the cost covered by insurance. The US News and World Report has consistently ranked Denmark as the best country in the world for women to live in. In 2016, it was the second best country to raise children and fourth on Save the Children's sixteenth annual Mother's Index, which assesses the well-being of mothers and children in 179 countries. Denmark came tenth in the overall list of the world's best countries.

We must put our pride aside and ask, what are those countries doing right that we ourselves can implement? When we want to learn a new skill, we take classes, read books, hire a coach, or watch YouTube videos. When we want to lose weight, we seek trainers, dietitians, or model men and women's formulas that consist of a highly effective regiment. The United States imported $2.409 trillion worth of goods from around the globe in 2017. We import tablets and iPhones from China; oil, machinery and vehicles from Canada; computers from Mexico; gems from India; and wine from France. Why not import lifestyle ideas that could benefit us as individuals, couples, families, communities, and as a nation?

If we look at gender equality as a whole, it appears overwhelming, a never-ending problem. The size and history of it seems discouraging. But if we bring it home and contain it within ourselves, we can begin with the basics, simply by following Socrates' advice: "Know thyself." Socrates said that people make themselves appear ridiculous when they try to know obscure things before they know themselves. Plato also alluded to the fact that understanding "thyself" would have a better impact on understanding the nature of a human being. But people today don't invest their time in introspection, and when they don't make that investment, they will not recognize fear-based, self-sabotaging behavior. They will not be able to treat themselves, let alone each other, with dignity.

Know thyself! People who rely solely on optimism will rob themselves of the energy required to take the necessary action to move forward. They refuse to do the work, even though without the reality, the work, they will endure incredible disappointments and will soon feel unmotivated and depleted. Their unfinished dreams are then passed on to the next generation. When we have too many dreams, and we've accumulated many unfinished dreams from one generation to the next, the task to achieve our dreams seems monumental and out of reach. This is especially the case if we are mothers, grandmothers, and caregivers who have devoted ourselves to the service of others. So we either never start taking steps toward achieving our dream or we stop before we reach our destination.

To manifest our dreams, we need to know ourselves, and to know ourselves we need to be grounded. Being grounded is important because it helps us understand who we are and what our purpose is on this earth. Being grounded helps us pull our heads out of the clouds, and with one foot in the physical world and the other foot in the spiritual world, keeps us well-rounded. It clarifies our purpose on this earth so that we're not simply dreamers floating around. We're actually living the dream. That's what Ninhursag was all about, and that's why she's called upon usually for fertility, either with procreation or gardening, and prayers related to the earth, nature, and being grounded.

Temple hymns identified her as the "true and great lady of heaven," perhaps because she stood on the mountain, and kings of Sumer were "nourished by Ninhursag's milk." Images on clay tablets depict her as confident and powerful. She sometimes had her hair in an omega shape and at other times she wore a horned headdress and tiered skirt. Oftentimes, she had bow cases at her shoulders and carried a mace or baton surmounted by an omega motif or a derivation, sometimes accompanied by a lion cub on a leash.

Ninhursag is the tutelary deity of several Sumerian leaders, meaning a spirit who is a guardian and protector of a particular place, lineage, nation, or culture. How do you remain grounded, a guardian of your thoughts and feelings, your home and family? Do you spend enough time with nature, watching the birds, squirrels, and other animals cross your path? Do you inhale the sweet perfumes of the woods, flowers, and air, and listen to the words and silence of God through mountains, water, trees, pastures, and countryside? Do you look for signs from nature to find your direction?

Everything alive has a language that is expressed through sounds and movements, that is alive and is expressing its own consciousness. The ancients talked to animals, trees, and the earth. It was considered a gift to do so, not a mental disorder. When we moved from the heart center to the brain complex, we lost the intuition to communicate with other living vibrations.

Nature is a tranquilizer. It refreshes your mind and body and creates mental clarity and peaceful concentration. Spend time in nature, in silence, and nurture your growth by regularly asking yourself, "What new habits do I need to acquire to make my dream possible? What habits must I let go of?" Make your list, and as you do so, breathe in gratitude, breathe out love, and give thanks for the perfect answer. As long as you remain grounded, you'll be able finish what Spirit has placed in your heart.

Chapter 4

Ningal
The Great Lady

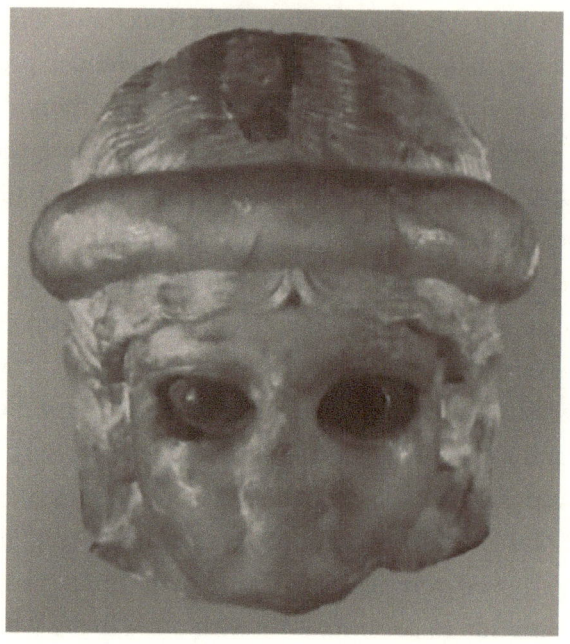

In the city of Ur, where the first settlements in the marshes of southern Mesopotamia were built with reeds without any type of nails or woods, Ningal was born to Ninhursag and Enki. Her name means the Great Lady, and she's also known as Nikkal.

As a young and pretty girl, she was the first to fall in love with Nanna, the moon god, when she sees him one evening soaring across the night skies. He happily responds by inviting her to meet him by the marshes. Although a bit shy, she cannot resist him. She joins Nanna at the marshes and the two spend many nights in secrecy enjoying a passionate and honey-mooned love.

One night, on the eve of the Dark Moon, Nanna says goodbye to Ningal, promising to return to her in two nights. He goes home to the skies, yet soon becomes impatient and descends to the Earth in disguise as a pilgrim, pleading for shelter. He knocks on Ningal's door and when she opens it, he begs her to join him in the marshes once again. By now, Ningal is a different woman. She has matured and is no longer as submissive as when they first met. This time, she is assertive and tells him to wait, explaining that he first must fulfill a set of wishes for her to continue with their relationship. Her requirements are not selfish, however, but are for the benefit of the fruitfulness of the land, of the marshes, of wild and domestic animals and their offspring.

Nanna obliges by doing as he has been asked, acknowledging Ningal as his true consort and beloved. True to her word, Ningal becomes his bride. In the tale, she evolves from the maiden bride of the moon god to the mother of the sun god Utu and her two daughters, Inanna/Ishtar, goddess of the planet Venus, and Ereshkigal, goddess of the underworld.

Ningal, the Sumerian and Akkadian goddess, is known as Nikkal in Phoenician and Aramaic. The oldest known song, written with both words and musical notation, comes from the remains of the ancient city of Ugarit in Syria. Written about 1400 BC, it's one of two hymns to the goddess Nikkal and to the seven goddesses of childbirth, the Kotharat, found in an ancient wedding myth. It's part of the story of Nikkal's marriage to the moon god. In the myth, he offers to pay her father a bride-price of a thousand shekels of silver and ten thousand of gold, along with some lapis lazuli. He promises to turn "the steppe land of her love into an orchard and vineyard." The language of the story is erotic.

Her father suggests that he marries two other goddesses, saying, "Oh most gracious of the gods, become son-in-law to Baal; wed Pidray his daughter. I shall introduce you to her father Baal. He will betroth you Yabradmay. His father's daughter Lion will arouse!"

But the moon god refuses. He says, "With Nikkal will be my wedding!"

Afterward he pays the bride-price for Nikkal.

The first part of Nikkal's wedding song recorded the courtship and payment of the bride-price, while the second half was concerned with the feminine aspects of the marriage, a hymn to the Kotharat, goddesses of pregnancy and childbirth. Fertility, symbolized by the birth of offspring, was believed to be the principal result of the marriage; thus, the Canaanites believed that fruitfulness in heaven would also result in terrestrial abundance for human beings. The story and song appear to be designed to be recited and performed as part of a wedding ritual. Ningal's symbol is a vessel of water with a fish in it, which signifies the womb, and it is in her womb that the sun god Utu is born along with his two sisters, Inanna/Ishtar.

Ningal was worshipped at Ur, especially during the period of the Third Dynasty. The kings of Ur III built her the temple E-karzida and dedicated statues and stele to her. While her story starts with love and marriage, it ends with her city's destruction. A poet wrote a song about the destruction of the city of Ur, around the time of the city's destruction in 2000 BC.

Lament for Ur is an ancient Sumerian rhythmical composition bewailing the collapse of the Third Dynasty of Ur. It's written in 436 lines and eleven songs, or stanzas, of unequal lengths and tells the terrible story which takes place both on earth and in the heavens. It begins by enumerating some of the prominent cities and temples of Sumer and the deities who had deserted them. In the second song, the people of Ur and other cities of Sumer are urged to rise and lament. The third song is about how the goddess Ningal hears the pleas of the people of Ur, but she is not able to dissuade the gods Anu and Enlil from their decision to destroy the city. The remaining songs relate the devastating results of Ur's defeat in battle. The last stanza ends with a plea to Ningal's husband, Nanna, that the city may once more rise up and that the people of Ur may again present their offerings to him.

The text is an example of the lament, a genre also exemplified in the Lamentations of the Bible, which is demonstrated in Mesopotamia from the Early Dynastic Period (2600-2340 BC) onward but flourished more particularly around 2000 BC, a time when the land witnessed several destructive invasions and wars broke out between the cities as they struggled for power after the fall of the Ur III Empire. Unlike most liturgical laments, with their stereotyped formulations, this is a very fine poem, composed and recited in response to a particular event: the destruction and rebuilding of the city of Ur. It tells of the decision of the great gods to allow the destruction of their temples and it describes the sack of the city and then reports the gods' final change of heart.

To date, five laments of this type have been identified and deciphered, each devoted to the destruction of a different city: the Ur Lament; the Sumer and Ur Lament; the Uruk Lament;

the Eridu Lament; and the Nippur Lament. The City Laments are characterized by vivid, rich descriptions of the destruction of the city, the mass killing of its inhabitants, and the loss of its central temple.

Dr. Uri Gabbay writes, "Shortly after the first Sumerian City Laments were deciphered in the early twentieth century, scholars began to notice their thematic and phraseological parallels to the biblical book of Lamentations. For instance, the deportee goddess in the Ur Lament l. 360 cries, 'I am one who can find no rest' and an identical phrase (She found no rest) describes the exiled daughter of Zion in Lamentations 1:3."

Dr. Gabbay goes on to give other examples such as the reference to the lack of musicians in the destroyed city, which appears in both traditions:

Lamentations (5:14)		Ur Lament (356)
וּתְבָשׁ רַעֲשָׁמּ םיְנָקְז םָתָנִיגְּנִמ םיִרוּחַב	The old men are gone from the gate, The young men from their music.	They are no longer playing for you the šem and ala drums that gladden the heart, nor the tigi.

Both traditions also use the image of pitchers, or potsherds, as a metaphor for dying people:

Lamentations (4:2)		Ur Lament (211)
נַּב יָקָר םיִיאָלֻּסְמ ןֹויִצ יֵנְבּ זָפַּב שָׂרָח יֵלְבִנְל וּבְשְׁחֶנ הָכיֵא רֵצוֹי יֵדְי הֵשֲׂעַמ	The precious children of Zion; Once valued as gold—Alas, they are accounted as earthen pots, Work of a potter's hands!	Its people littered its sides like potsherds.

Another famous example is the "fox in the ruins" image, which is shared by the biblical and Sumerian lament traditions:

Mesopotamian Goddesses

Lamentations (5:17)		Ur Lament (269)
עַל הַר־צִיּוֹן שֶׁשָּׁמֵם שׁוּעָלִים הִלְּכוּ־בוֹ	Because of Mount Zion, which lies desolate; Foxes walk over it.	In the rivers of my city, dust has gathered, fox-holes are made therein

Ningal tells how she suffered.

LAMENT FOR UR

For the gods have abandoned us
like migrating birds they have gone
Ur is destroyed, bitter is its lament
The country's blood now fills its holes like hot bronze in a mould
Bodies dissolve like fat in the sun. Our temple is destroyed
Smoke lies on our city like a shroud
blood flows as the river does
the lamenting of men and women
sadness abounds
Ur is no more

Most scholars date the destruction of Ur, in ancient Chaldea, to a time period when the Elamites conquered the Sumerians, ending their civilization. Some have suggested that these laments, since they don't mention battles or conquering armies but rather a fury of natural forces commanded by vengeful gods, refer to earlier events, the first two chapters of the book of Abraham that describe the destruction of the Tower of Babel and the Confusion of Tongues.

Ningal is associated with dream divination, vision, and interpretation. It's believed that the world's first book of dreams, a collection of dream symbols and their meanings, comes from Mesopotamia. Sumerians observed their dreams as signs and messages sent from gods. People had their dreams translated by "dream priests" who projected the dreamer's future. The method of planting and nurturing dreams, then bidding them into reality by means of special rituals is thought to have been invented during this period. These practices then spread throughout the ancient world and endured in countless formulas until the twentieth century. Some believe that the Mesopotamian model of dream interpretation had an impact on the cultural beliefs of the Egyptians and gave rise to the Hebrew, Arabic, and Greek traditions of dream interpretation.

Life is more than the physical realm. Most people experience the spirit world, God's communication with us, in countless ways such as through situations, wise guidance, people, thoughts, supernatural manifestations, silence, and dreams and visions. The opportunity to speak and listen to God helps build our self-esteem, a belief in ourselves that is difficult to break, and yet, although women are generally more religious than men, they're more prone to self-worth issues. Today, lack of confidence affects a lot of women, even those in leadership roles. Could this be tied to thousands of years of a not-so-pleasant story of her gender's spiritual abilities, not to mention the history of what happened to women who acted upon their female mysticism?

In the four centuries from 1400 to 1800, several European and North American countries were troubled by the specter of the witch. The persecution of accused witches in Europe resulted in trial and sometimes torture and execution of tens of thousands of victims, about 80 percent of whom were women, according to historian Brian Levack. Under the guidance of the *Malleus Maleficarum*, or the Hammer of the Witches, millions of women were declared heretics and tortured, hung, or burned alive during the infamous witch hunts. This female genocide targeted any woman with property or power, women who practiced herbal or natural forms of healing (midwives in particular), and women who displayed sexual independence.

A study conducted by anthropologists in one Chinese region provided an opportunity to test the most common hypothesis, that witchcraft accusations act as punishments for those who do not cooperate with local norms. According to this theory, witch tags mark supposedly untrustworthy individuals and encourage others to conform out of fear of being labeled. However, some empirical studies have shown that witch labeling instead undermines trust and social cohesion in a society.

Louise Jackson notes that the confessions made by the Suffolk women charged with witchcraft in 1645 indicate that, in many cases, accused women were contextualizing their own experiences within a wider demonological framework. Often they were judging themselves in their roles as wives and mothers—the witch, after all, was the behavioral opposite of the stereotypical role model of the "good wife." There are noticeable references to infanticide, suicide, and possible abuse. It could well be that women who possessed no other language to describe certain traumatic experiences took on the conceptual framework of demonology as a way of explaining events. Witch-hunting was a method of behavioral control in which women as victims (in many senses of the word) were themselves participating because they had no other framework of reference.

Author Karlene T. Clark explains that, by definition, a witch is an adherent of wicca. The word wicca, female and pronounced witcha, or wicce, male and pronounced witcheh, are old Anglo-Saxon words that meant "to know" or "wise one." The word became synonymous with "witch" due to interpretations and misunderstandings. The original wicca were the herb florists, the women who knew how to use natural things like plants, tree bark, and flowers to treat pain and illness. There was no magic involved.

When Rome created medical schools and started switching to a male-only practice, they wanted to do away with the wise women who took away business by creating simples and tinctures. They went to the church and received a papal bull document that gave them permission to seek out "witches."

During the rise of female mysticism, female spirituality became criminalized and women were increasingly persecuted by the Church. Gaia Cloutier writes, "The most central tenet of mysticism is that through a combination of physical, ritual, intellectual, and spiritual practices it is possible for the individual soul of the mystic to achieve an encounter with God."

Jesus, considered the greatest mystic, realized that all beings are manifestations of the divine. His goal was to bring people close to God, to the point of each person becoming one with God, which is the essence of mysticism. In John 10:30, Jesus said, "I and the Father are one" and "The kingdom of God is within you" (Luke 17:21). In John 10:31-34, he clearly declares to a group of Jews that they are also gods. When his Jewish opponents picked up stones to stone him, he said to them, "I have shown you many good works from the

Father. For which of these do you stone me?"

"We are not stoning you for any good work," they replied, "but for blasphemy, because you, a mere man, claim to be God."

Jesus answered them, "Is it not written in your Law, I have said you are also gods?"

Jesus also said, in John 14:12, "I tell you the truth, anyone who has faith in me will do what I have been doing. He will do even greater things than these, because I am going to the Father."

While it may be difficult to imagine anyone performing miracles more extraordinary than the ones Jesus performed, that's what Jesus believed we're capable of. A rebellious teacher, he argued against dogmatism and used metaphors and parables to point to higher, more intangible and universal truths. He was able in all situations to both validate and confirm the wisdom that he conveyed. His ability to perform miracles also supports itself with abilities we are all said to have once enlightenment transpires.

Cloutier writes that "Many female mystics were able to live meaningful, productive, and fulfilling lives throughout the medieval period and were viewed as holy or authoritative by their communities and the Church. Other mystics, however, instead occupied ambiguous space between safely orthodox and dangerously heterodox in the eyes of the Church and their communities. The Church had a number of concerns about the dangerous potential of mystics."

Fears regarding women's spiritual powers exist in all religious books which focus on a male God, male prophets, male disciples, male messengers and miracle makers, with few women worthy of prominence mention. Most women in these books are cast as the devil's gateway, accused of causing trouble for the world and suffering as a result—whether through the pain of pregnancies, oppression, or violence. Of the 124,000 or so supreme humans responsible for reforming their people and bringing them toward God, Muhammad being the final messenger, the Quran does not mention any female prophets.

Religions raise the rank of men over women, have stricter sanctions against women, and require them to be submissive, dismissing their supernatural powers even though, in general and as less egotistical child-bearers, women are more attuned to the spiritual, unseen world.

Spirituality requires that one uses their intuition, and that means being in touch with our feelings. Almost all religions emphasize feelings rather than thinking. This is the way to grace and sacred knowledge.

Today, the spirit of Ningal's teachings survives. Today, you see a rebirth of "witches" because people have rediscovered that our Earth needs us to protect it, that the magic of the natural world has many remedies with few side effects, and there is a balance in the duality of the faith. Today, a woman can honor her dreams and visions. By responding to her calling, she can shine bright and carry the light for others.

The power of dreaming has been destroyed in ancient Mesopotamia, forced to travel to other parts of the world, like the United States, where the indigenous people of this land have nurtured it and kept it alive for thousands of years. People from around the world risk their life to come to America to make their dreams come true, understanding that there's more to life than just the physical realm.

Inside each one of us is a place where time doesn't exist and perceptions surpass the limits of the physical and material world. That's where our visions and dreams live. But in a world bombarded with noise and a consumer-oriented environment, how do we activate that part of us? One technique is to understand and awaken your third eye.

The third eye is a mystical and esoteric concept referring to the ajna chakra. It is a speculative invisible eye which provides perception beyond ordinary sight and acts as a spiritual gateway. The third eye is associated with clairvoyance, out-of-body experiences, visions, and precognition. People who have developed their third eye are known as seers.

Everyone has access to their third eye. When you have a hunch and act on it, you've used your third eye. Your third eye is a sense which can be advanced to be more refined and accurate than just being a hunch. When you work on your third eye, you open up your imagination, tap into your innermost dreams, become aware, and understand the metaphysics of your own existence. Your eating habits might change and so will your hearing as you become more attuned to the sounds of nature.

What does the Bible say about the third eye? According to Matthew 6:22-23, "For where your treasure is, there your heart will be also. The eye is the lamp of the body. If your vision is clear, your whole body will be full of light. But if your vision is poor, your whole body will be full of darkness. If then the light within you is darkness, how great is that darkness!"

There are many ways to advance your third eye, including resting under the moon, sitting against a tree bark, cultivating silence, nurturing your creativity, practicing contemplation, journaling, and dream work which includes writing and interpreting your dreams.

How will you use your dreams in this world?

Think of this poem by Steve Maraboli.

> Cemeteries are full of unfulfilled dreams... countless echoes of "could have" and "should have"... countless books unwritten... countless songs unsung... I want to live my life in such a way that when my body is laid to rest, it will be a well needed rest from a life well lived, a song well sung, a book well written, opportunities well explored, and a love well expressed.

Chapter 5

Inanna and Ereshkigal
Goddess of Heaven and Earth
Goddess of the Underworld

Inanna, the daughter of Ningal and Enki, is the most beloved and revered goddess of the Sumerians. Ishtar is Inanna's name in Akkadian. Both names bear the title "Queen of Heaven and Earth." Inanna's story begins with *The Huluppu-Tree*, a hymn which has many similarities to the creation of genesis.

> In the first days, in the very first days,
> In the first nights, in the very first nights,
> In the first years, in the very first years,
>
> In the first days when everything needed was brought into being,
> In the first days when everything needed was properly nourished,

When bread was baked in the shrines of the land,
And bread was tasted in the homes of the land,
When heaven had moved away from earth,
And the earth had separated from heaven,
And the name of man was fixed;
When the Sky God, An, had carried off the heavens,
And the Air God, Enlil, had carried off the earth,
When the Queen of the Great Below, Ereshkigal, was given the underworld for her domain.

It's in this hymn that Inanna is introduced as a young lady in search of her womanhood. It all starts with a huluppu-tree, the willow, planted mysteriously by the banks of the Euphrates. When the whirling south wind rises, it pulls its roots and rips at its branches until the waters of the river carry it away. Inanna finds the tree and plucks it from the river, saying, "I shall bring this tree to Uruk. I shall plant this tree in my holy garden."

Inanna cares for the tree with her hand and settles the earth around the tree with her foot. She wonders, "How long will it be until I have a shining throne to sit upon? How long will it be until I have a shining bed to lie upon?" Years pass, five, then ten, and the tree grows thick without its bark splitting.

One day, a serpent comes along and makes its nest in the roots of the tree. Inanna tries to charm it away but to no avail. Then the Anzu-bird sets its young in the tree branches and the dark maid Lilith builds her home in the trunk. Inanna, who loves to laugh, suddenly begins to weep and weep and weep. Still, the serpent, bird, and Lilith refuse to leave the tree.

At the coming of dawn, the birds begin to sing and Inanna calls out to her brother Utu, the sun god, who just awoke and left his royal bedchamber. She says, "Oh Utu, in the days when the fates were decreed, when abundance overflowed in the land, when the Sky God took the heavens and the Air God the earth, when Ereshkigal (Inanna's sister) was given the Great Below for her domain, the God of Wisdom, Father Enki, set sail for the underworld, and the underworld rose up and attacked him… At that time, a tree, a single tree, the huluppa-tree was planted by the banks of the Euphrates. The South Wind pulled at its roots and ripped its branches until the water of the Euphrates carried it away. I plucked the tree from the river; I brought it to my holy garden. I tended the tree, waiting for my shining throne and bed."

Inanna goes on to explain how the serpent who couldn't be charmed made its nest in the root of the tree, that the Anzu-bird set his young in the branches of the tree, and that the dark maid Lilith built her home in the trunk. She explains how she wept, and wept, and wept, but they would not leave her tree. Utu, the warrior, listens yet refuses to help his sister, so the next morning, she calls to her brother Gilgamesh. She explains the whole story and this brother decides to help her. He fastens his armor of sixty pounds around his chest, which to him felt as light as the weight of fifty feathers. He lifts over his shoulder his bronze axe, which weighs 450 pounds, and enters Inanna's holy garden.

Gilgamesh strikes the serpent, which causes the Anzu-bird to fly away with his young to the mountains and Lilith to smash her home and flee to the wild, uninhabited places. He then loosens the roots of the huluppa-tree and with the help of the men who accompanied him, cuts off the branches. From the trunk of the tree he carves a throne and bed for his holy sister. From the roots of the tree she fashions a pukku and a mikku for Gilgamesh, the hero of Uruk who helped make Inanna's dream come true. Unfortunately, he ends up losing the gifts she gives him because he isn't mature enough to use them wisely, but instead, uses them to cause the mothers, sisters, and young maidens of Uruk to feel bitterness and lamentation. So the earth opens up and sucks the items into the underworld.

In this story, the masculine Gilgamesh works together with the feminine Inanna to help her achieve her dream. The powers of the masculine and feminine cannot live without the other. A feminine and masculine marriage within ourselves and our relationships helps set a sacred spiritual life into motion. The feminine aspects that embrace intuition, creativity, compassion, receptivity, and nurturing need the masculine aspects that embrace logic, decisiveness, and action, and vice versa.

The imbalances of the feminine and masculine within individuals is the cause of people jumping from one relationship to the next in search of that person who will balance them. People place a great amount of focus on the idea of two people falling in love and getting married. Couples get so caught up in the romanticism of marriage that they expect their wedding day to be the happiest day of their lives. What, then, of the thousands of days that follow? They expect their spouse to be the perfect mate and fulfill their needs when really, our partner is there to hold a mirror for us and show us what we still need to heal and how to continue to grow.

The Western world's emphasis on love is massive. With ads and campaigns for Valentine's Day, Christmas, Sweetest Day, birthdays, wedding anniversaries, and on and on, you'd think the world would have figured out how to live happily ever after. Instead, the divorce rate in the United States is about 40 to 50 percent and in other countries the numbers are much higher.

As a result of excessive romanticism, love has become a constipated condition. Couples tend to take their spouse too seriously and not take their marriage seriously enough. The sacred union of marriage was created as a stable structure meant to give people the opportunity to gracefully enjoy sex and procreation and to ensure that the child or children born as a result will have a stable environment to be raised in. Like all unions, marriage requires that we give up parts of our freedom in exchange for other freedoms. Doing what's necessary for the higher good requires courage and mastery and it provides enormous long-term rewards.

Indian Yogi and bestselling author Sadhguru says that a new life, a child, needs a maximum amount of support and, above all else, a stable situation. "Whether you like it or not, it's a minimum twenty-year project," he said, adding that a person who chooses to get married should choose consciously. "This [divorce] is a completely American idea. Nobody thought of divorce in this country until recently. If it happens, something went truly wrong and the couple separated, that will anyway inevitably happen. You don't have to plan it at the time of the wedding. Why should you talk about marriage and divorce at the same time? It's a crime."

Divorce starts in the mind. It's perpetuated by examples we witness and images we see in the media. From childhood, we watch and read fairytales that depict an unrealistic portrait of happiness and love. Happily ever after doesn't just happen. Like writing a book, raising a family, or building a new home or business, it requires years of work and commitment.

The way to honor our marriage is to remember why we married the person to begin with, and re-remember, and so on down the years. By constantly remembering why we married our spouse, we retreat and recover our strength and energy. Every so often, we also need to ask ourselves, what mirror is my partner holding up for me? What story is he or she helping me heal? What dreams and visions do I have for us? How will I manifest those dreams and visions without infringing upon my partner's growth? How can I change my life, reach my goals, and still keep my partner in my life?

Inanna and the God of Wisdom

Now that Inanna has been given the confidence and courage to take action, she puts on her crown and acknowledges the beauty of her womanhood by going to the sheepfold, leaning against the apple tree, and rejoicing at her wondrous vulva. She decides to visit Enki, her grandfather, the god of wisdom, in the city of Eridu, located where the Tigris and Euphrates rivers meet with the Persian Gulf.

Enki senses her arrival and gives these instructions to his

minister Isimud. "When Inanna enters the holy shrine, give her butter cake to eat. Pour cold water to refresh her heart. Offer her beer before the statue of the lion. Treat her like an equal. Greet Inanna at the holy table, the table of heaven."

Isimud does as he's told, and afterward, Enki and Inanna drink beer together, and drink more beer, and drink more beer, their bronze vessels filled to overflowing. They toast and challenge each other and, one by one, Enki begins to give her the *me*, the Sumerian holy laws of heaven and earth, declaring, "In the name of my power! In the name of my holy shrine! To my daughter Inanna I shall give the high priesthood! Godship! The noble, enduring crown! The throne of kingship!"

Inanna replies, "I take them!"

He goes on with the same heartfelt oaths and gives her the descent into the underworld and the ascent from the underworld; the love of art making; the kissing of the phallus.

She replies, "I take them!"

He continues with his toasts, raising his cup, and declares he'll give her the holy priestess of heaven; the setting up of lamentations; the rejoicing of the heart; the giving of judgments; the making of decisions. Fourteen times he offers his granddaughter the holy *me*, and fourteen times she accepts and acknowledges the long list of what he gave her which contains the dagger and sword, the black garment, the colorful garment, the loosening of the hair, the binding of the hair, the quiver, the art of lovemaking, the art of forthright speech, the art of slanderous speech, the art of adorning speech, the resounding musical instrument, the art of song, hero, power, treachery, kindness and many more, including the sexual rituals. He gave her the craft of woodworker, copper worker, scribe, smith, leather maker, and on and on. He even gave her the emotions of fear, consternation, and dismay.

After he finishes giving her all the *me*, to which she'd replied, "I take them," he tells his minister to make sure that after she leaves, she safely reaches her city Uruk. Inanna gathers all the *me*, places them on the Boat of Heaven, and pushes it off from the dock. Once sober, Enki looks around and notices all the *me* are missing. He calls on his minister and asks him where are the high priesthood and godship, the noble enduring crown, the art of the hero and the art of power, of treachery and deceit?

Isimud responds, "My king has given them to his daughter."

Fourteen times Enki questions his minister and fourteen times he receives the same answer, with Isimud finally explaining that all the *me* have been given to Inanna. Coming to his senses, Enki demands that Isimud bring back the Boat of Heaven to Eridu. Isimud obeys and goes with this message to Inanna. "My king has said: 'Let Inanna proceed to Uruk; Bring the Boat of Heaven with the holy *me* back to Eridu.'"

Inanna, heartbroken, cries, "My father has changed his word to me! He has violated his pledge—broken his promise! Deceitfully my father spoke to me!"

But she's not dejected for long. She calls her servant Ninshubur, requesting her to save the Boat of Heaven. So Ninshubur slices the air with her hand and with her thunderous cry drives the creatures that Isimud had brought along back to Eridu. When Enki finds out what happened, he tells him to take fifty uru-giants this time to seize the Boat of Heaven and bring it back to Eridu. Ninshubur is once again able to rescue the boat which is now getting closer and closer to Uruk. Enki realizes he must move quickly and tells Isimud to take with him fifty lahama-monsters to bring back the boat. But even they aren't able to withstand Ninshubur's protection of the boat. This went on a fourth, fifth, and sixth time, with Enki's creatures, giants, and monsters failing to bring back the boat.

Having triumphed, Ninshubur tells Inanna that when the boat enters the gate of Uruk to let high water flow in the city and to let the deep-going boats sail swiftly through the canals. Inanna agrees to this and adds other beautiful blessings,

> On the day the Boat of Heaven
> Enters the Nigulla Gate of Uruk,
> Let high water sweep over the streets;
> Let high water flow over the paths.
> Let the old men give counsel;
> Let the old women offer heart-soothing.
> Let the young men show the might of their weapons;
> Let the children laugh and sing.
> Let all of Uruk be festive!
> Let the high priest greet the Boat of Heaven with song.
> Let him utter great prayers.
> Let the king slaughter oxen and sheep.
> Let him pour beer out of the cup.
> Let the drum and tambourine resound.
> Let the sweet tigi—music be played.
> Let all the lands proclaim my noble name.
> Let my people sing my praises.
> And so it was.

The boat docks and the holy *me* are unloaded and presented to the people of Sumer. More *me* appear, providing additional gifts for the people. Inanna brings allure, the art of women, the perfect execution of the *me*. The people graciously accept the *me,* and when Enki realizes that Inanna's intent wasn't just to keep the powers for herself, he blesses the process, saying, "In the name of my power! In the name of my holy shrine! Let the *me* you have taken with you remain in the holy shrine of your city. Let the high priest spend his day at the holy shrine in song. Let the citizens of your city prosper. Let the children of Uruk rejoice!"

Many women feel empty because they don't know what they want. What the media, their friends, and the world tell them will give them a productive and fulfilling life isn't really working. It's a generic, sometimes even pathetic, image of a good life. It's difficult to know what we want when we're being bombarded with so many messages and responsibilities. The fear of stepping out of the circle of friends and relatives who live a conventional lifestyle can also numb our deepest wants and desires until we arrive to a point where we can no longer fake the emptiness and we finally have the courage to step into our truths.

Inanna knew what she wanted, power, and she wasn't ashamed or afraid to ask for it. She then received it with great poise and confidence. Knowing exactly what to do with this power, she carried it in a boat to her city. She shared it and helped her people with it. Inanna believed in herself and, contrary to Cinderella, Sleeping Beauty, and Snow White, the famous girl stories we grew up with, she wasn't abused by a step-sister or a stranger, not rescued by a man, wasn't kissed in her sleep, and her ability to attain power and serve the world wasn't dependent on a prince. Inanna wasn't the damsel in distress. She was the heroine of her own destiny, had a purpose in life greater than herself, and she didn't hesitate to serve that purpose and her people.

A woman is a source of infinite inspiration, transformation, and power. She can do wonders if she simply trusts herself and her femininity and doesn't clone herself as a man to make things happen. She can educate herself in matters that concern her and her family. Whether through formal institutions or self-taught methods, she can become an expert and succeed in her field. She can take part in politics, community work, be a leader, and run a well-organized company, home, and garden. Honoring her work and performing her best is important in the kitchen as well as in the office. All work is sacred and when treated as an act of love will not feel like work at all.

I've lived by a formula I learned decades ago from author Dr. Joseph Murphy that resembles Inanna's course of actions. He wrote that there are three steps to success: The first step is to find out the thing you love to do, then do it; the second step is to specialize in some particular branch of work and learn more about it than anyone else; the third and most important step is to be sure that the thing you want to do does not lead to your success only. Your desire must not be selfish; it must benefit humanity.

What do you love to do? Have you invested enough time, energy, and money into learning all you could about it? Does your desire have a service component to it? How will it help others? Do you have the courage to step into the world and own your craft? What do you need to do, to get rid of or possess, to feel ready for the next step?

The Courtship of Inanna and Dumuzi

The courtship of Inanna and Dumuzi, sometimes compared to the Song of Solomon, is one of the oldest love poems. The story starts off with Inanna and her older brother, the sun god Utu, chatting poetically about preparing her bridal sheets. Utu wants to help prepare her for her marriage by bringing her linen. She asks him who will comb, spin, braid, weave, and bleach the linen after he brings it? He offers to comb, spin, braid, weave, and bleach the linen. So she asks him, "After you've brought my bridal sheet to me, who will go to bed with me?"

"Sister, your bridegroom will go to bed with you." He goes on to tell her that Dumuzi will go to bed with her.

She's not pleased with this. She doesn't want the shepherd to be her bridegroom. She wants the farmer. She says the farmer is the man of her heart, adding, "He gathers the grain into great heaps. He brings the grain regularly into my storehouses."

Her brother urges her to marry the shepherd, and asks, "Why are you unwilling? His cream is good; his milk is good. Whatever he touches shines brightly. Dumuzi will share his rich cream with you. You who are meant to be the king's protector. Why are you unwilling?"

Inanna refuses, insists that she will not marry the shepherd, whose clothes are coarse and whose wool is rough. She wants to marry the farmer, who grows flax for her clothes and barley for her table. These words move Dumuzi and he speaks, appearing into the story like an eagle in the sky. He asks, "Why do you speak about the farmer? Why do you speak about him? If he gives you black flour, I will give you black wool. If he gives you white flour, I will give you white wool. If he gives you beer, I will give you sweet milk. If he gives you bread, I will give you honey cheese. I will give the farmer my leftover cream. I will give the farmer my leftover milk. What does he have more than I do?"

"Shepherd, without my mother, Ningal, you'd be driven away," says Inanna. "Without my grandmother, Ningikuga, you'd be driven into the steeps. Without my father, Nanna, you'd have no roof. Without my brother Utu…"

"Inanna, do not start a quarrel," says Dumuzi. "My father Enki is as good as your father Nanna. My mother Sirtur is as good as your mother Ningal. My sister Geshtinanna is as good as yours. Queen of the palace, let us talk it over."

The word they had spoken
Was a word of desire.
From the starting of the quarrel
Came the lovers' desire.

The shepherd goes to the royal house with cream and milk, stands in front of the door and calls out, "Open the house, my lady, open the house!"

Inanna runs to her mother, Ningal, for counsel. Ningal tells her, "My child, the young man will be your father. My daughter, the young man will be your mother. He will treat you like a father. He will care for you like a mother. Open the house, my lady, open the house!"

Inanna listens to her mother's counsel. She bathes and anoints herself with scented oil and covers her body with the royal white robe. She prepares her dowry and arranges her precious lapis beads around her neck and takes her seal in her hand. All the while, Dumuzi waits expectantly until finally, Inanna opens the door.

> Inside the house she shone before him.
> Like the light of the moon.
> Dumuzi looked at her joyously.
> He pressed his neck close against hers.
> He kissed her.

Inanna requests that the bed that rejoices the heart and sweetens the loins, the bed of kingship and queenship, the royal bed, be prepared. She spreads the bridal sheet across the bed and says to Dumuzi, "What I tell you let the singer weave into song. What I tell you, let it flow from ear to mouth. Let it pass from old to young." She speaks,

> My vulva, the horn,
> The Boat of Heaven
> Is full of eagerness like the young moon.

My untilled land lies fallow.
As for me, Inanna,
Who will plow my vulva?
Who will plow my high field?
Who will plow my wet ground?
As for me, the young woman,
Who will plow my vulva?
Who will station the ox there?
Who will plow my vulva?

Dumuzi says that he, the king, will plow her vulva, and she accepts, saying, "Then plow my vulva, many of my heart! Plow my vulva!"

He sweeps her into his love and says to her, "Oh Lady, your breast is your field, Inanna. Your broad field pours out plants and grains. Water and bread flows from on high from your servant. Pour it out for me, Inanna, and I will drink all you offer!"

"The shepherd Dumuzi filled my lap with cream and milk, stroked my pubic hair, watered my womb, laid his hands on my holy vulva, smoothed my black boat with cream, quickened my narrow boat with milk, caressed me on the bed. Now I will caress my high priest on the bed…"

Inanna goes on with romantic and erotic details about her relationship with her husband, promising to watch over his house of life, the storehouse, "the shining quivering place which delights Sumer. The house which decides the fates of the land. The house which gives breath of life to the people. I, the queen of the palace, will watch over your house." She decrees a sweet fate for him, further promising, "In battle I am your leader. In combat I am your armor-bearer. In the assembly I am your advocate. On the campaign I am your inspiration."

Inanna accepts him to rule the land as her consort. The couple continues with their lovemaking, with rich images and a succulent sexual experience that indicates the land will be fruitful because of their union. At the end, Dumuzi asks to be set free, to go and take his place as king. So she sets him free.

The relationship between Inanna and Dumuzi is evidence of a time when the Feminine Divine was respected and revered, where women and not just men ruled the land and made eminent decisions for their people. In this love story, Inanna portrays confidence and a full embrace of her womanhood. She and Dumuzi have a mutual, natural, and healthy attitude toward intimacy. There isn't the language of rape and abuse, nor are there bad or dirty thoughts about sex, which is found in later literature.

It is this very confidence and love for herself that caused the male gods, rulers, and writers in later years to attach negative qualities to her character. They changed the narrative and women began to forget their worthiness, creating a sexual wound that impacts girls from a very early age. The way to heal this wound is for each woman to honor herself, her worth, growth, and dreams, to celebrate her phases of menstruation, childbearing, and menopause, to be an example and break the pattern.

In some cultures, bed sheets are still inspected after a couple's wedding night to check for bloodstains that allegedly prove the bride's virginity. The virginity test was practiced in Western cultures during the Middle Ages. Brides throughout history have had the burden of coming up with clever ways to ensure that their sheets are stained with blood while their grooms have prized their promiscuity. Susan Kent writes that during the Victorian Era, no matter what the women desired, most were predestined to become wives due to their economic reliance on men. Secondly, to be even considered as a potential wife, women had to be not only virgins but were expected to remain innocent and free from any thought of love or sexuality until after they had received a proposal, a requirement not expected of men.

"If you read the witch trial accounts, it's all about sexuality being this horrible, dangerous force," says Starhawk, a witch, activist, and one of the founding mothers of neo-Goddess religion. This would explain why television forbids sex but welcomes extreme violence. By covering it up, films make it clear that sex is negative. Violence, on the other hand, is so glorified that its levels of goriness goes up a notch regularly.

Here's an example. One night as I flipped through the channels, I came across a scene in the movie *Wrong Turn* where four gruesome men kill and slice people with hammers, lawnmowers, butcher knives, and axes. None of the gory scenes in *Wrong Turn* were edited except for the nipples of a dead woman. Her nipples were hazed as her corpse hung naked upside down while one of the killers decapitated her. *Wrong Turn* is a series of nine films with a strong following and it's considered by box office standards to be a great success.

The Middle East also has its dose of violent films and news channels which focus on morals that normally doesn't serve women. In 2014, Egypt banned the Egyptian-made movie, *Beauty of the Soul*, for scenes deemed sexually provocative. The film, starring famous Lebanese singer Haifa Wehbe, was inspired by Monica Bellucci's 2000 hit *Malena*. In an interview, the director of the film asked those who helped in the decision to ban the film if they had ever seen it. They responded, "No, but we saw the ad."

"If you are going to ban a movie, couldn't you have at least watched it first?" he asked in frustration.

"Do I have to smoke a cigarette in order to know whether or not it's bad for you?" answered one of the officials.

Ironically, breasts are a natural thing that almost everyone sees in real life every day. God made them for a divine purpose. They feed and nourish babies. Violence, rape, and killing are the exact opposite of what breasts represent, yet the breasts are seen as a threat to society's eyes, even when a woman is breastfeeding, while violence is seen as a safe zone, with the philosophy that viewers know it's fake and therefore it's harmless—even though for decades, the American Psychiatric Association and the American Medical Association have both made unequivocal statements about the link between media violence and violence in our society. Research on violent television and films, video games, and music reveals unequivocal evidence that media violence increases the likelihood of aggressive and violent behavior in both immediate and long-term contexts.

Conrad Hilton was right. In his biography, he mentions how he had tried to ban or lessen violence from TV shows but realized he was not going to see it happen in his lifetime. He died in 1979. It's interesting how most people would agree that sex is good, natural, and created to do the most beautiful thing in the world, procreation, and most people would agree that violence is bad and unnatural. Yet since biblical times, stories of violence have been treated as more of a norm while sex has been treated with disapproval.

For a woman to take control of her sexual health, she needs to celebrate her body and know who she is in relation to other people and situations in her life. To start, she could at times remove herself from worldly things, including sexual activity, to listen to her emotional and physical wants and needs. People have forgotten the importance associated with being alone, which is especially important during menstruation, a powerful time which allows a woman to reconnect with herself and her spirituality. Menstruation is not an indication of uncleanliness or impurity, as most religions view it. It's not a curse or an inconvenience that should be described with exasperated descriptions such as "Oh, it's that time of the month." It ought to be an honored and nurturing time because a woman's period is when she cleanses and clears herself of old energies from the past month.

Through her menstruation, a woman is also cleansing and clearing old energies for her family by taking on the emotions of the men and children around her and transforming that into the blood which she then sheds. Once it's over, she's strong again and she returns to her regular activities with inspiration, a new perspective and energy. Women's hormones protect her health but hormones are not as able to do so when she tries to become too masculine or when, due to loneliness or the need for acceptance, she permits men to use her body in disrespectful sexual activities.

Another way for a woman to take control of her sexual health is to have the courage to share with society a new perspective that would cause a huge paradigm shift in how we view things. For example, we are inundated with the idea that, because women bear the consequences of sex, they must be primarily responsible for preventing pregnancy. In a twitter thread that went viral, Gabrielle Blair wrote that she'd written the thread for several months but had been hesitant to share it, adding, "Not sure why. But hearing so many men talking about women's rights (related to the Kavanaugh hearings), brought me to hit publish." Blair posed the question, "What could we do as a society to have men shoulder the burden of preventing unwanted pregnancies?"

She wrote that she'd been listening to men grandstand about women's reproductive rights, and she was convinced that men, who mostly run our government and mostly make the laws, actually have zero interest in stopping abortion. She made a long list of why people should stop trying to control women's bodies and sexuality because unwanted pregnancies were caused by men. She wrote, among many, many things, that all men had to do to eliminate abortions in three months or less, without ever touching an abortion law or even mentioning women, was to simply use condoms or pull out. She wrote, "Don't put women at risk. Don't choose to maximize your own pleasure if it risks causing women pain." She adds that while modern birth control is possibly the greatest invention of the last century, it's also brutal with side effects and for many women ridiculously harmful. Also, some form of women's birth control is harder to get and more expensive. And she points out that while women might get pregnant two days out of a month, which makes twenty-four days a year, men can cause pregnancy 365 days out of the year.

Much of what Gabrielle said is true and thought provoking, and it's not meant to remove responsibility from women in cases of consensual sex. But for thousands of years, society has placed the burden on her because she's the one who has to carry a child, face an abortion, raise the child, and chase after financial assistance if the man decides not to acknowledge the child or participate in its life.

While we've come a long way, in most countries society is still very hard on women. We women are even hard on ourselves. But we'll continue to be in the shadow of victimhood if we blame others for our current situations.

My Native American teachers once asked me to make a list of ten sentences that start with "I am" and then fill in the blank. During that time, I was single and wanted to get married, knew this was in my future but, for some reason, there seemed to be countless obstacles. I did the assignment and, looking over my list of "I am" statements, I noticed I'd claimed that I am a daughter, sister, writer, and other adjectives, but I'd placed "lover" at the lower part of the list. I might have been too ashamed to claim what I really wanted.

Suddenly it dawned on me that my priorities were not in the right order. Afraid of my own desires, I was giving Spirit mixed messages and therefore continued to live first and foremost as a daughter, sister, writer, etc. I rewrote the list, rearranging the order of my roles, placing "lover/wife" at the top. In doing so, I shifted from the past of who I once was to the future of who I wanted to become. That exercise, along with a lot of other energy work, helped me connect with my husband shortly afterward.

Create a list of ten sentences that start with "I am…" and fill in the blank. See where your priorities are today and consider switching the numerical order or adding desires you've neglected to identify if you want to see yourself playing a different role in the future. Then spend time every day imagining this role, feeling and acting it out, until the power of your imagination gracefully blossoms like a flower and brings a new fragrance into your life.

The Descent of Inanna

This story was originally written in cuneiform (between 3500 BC and 1900 BC or even earlier) and inscribed on clay tablets as a poem, filled with meaning, symbolism, and numerous interpretations.

From the great heaven she set her mind on the great below.
From the great heaven the goddess set her mind on the great below.
From the great heaven Inanna set her mind on the great below.
My mistress abandoned heaven, abandoned earth, and descended to the underworld.
Inanna abandoned heaven, abandoned earth, and descended to the underworld.

Now that her husband is off being king, Inanna leaves

everything behind and journeys to the underground, where her sister Ereshkigal reigns. She takes seven of the *me*, divine powers she used for protection, and prepares for the journey. She places a crown on her head, arranges a wig across her forehead, hangs small lapis lazuli beads around her neck, and wears double strands of beads over her breasts. She wraps the royal robe around her body, daubs eye ointment called "Let him come, let him come," binds the breastplate called "Come, man, come!" around her chest, and places a golden ring on her hand. She also takes the lapis measuring rod and line. She wears each of these adornments at the level of each Kundalini Chakra.

Before she goes on her journey, she tells her faithful minister Ninshubur that, in case she faces trouble and doesn't return, to lament her loss, beat the drum for her absence, to dress in a single garment like a beggar, and then go to the cities, circling the houses of the gods. She instructs her to first go to Enlil, her paternal grandfather, and crying, tell him not to let his daughter, Inanna, be put to death in the underworld. If he doesn't care to help, then, she tells Ninshubur, go to Nanna, her father, and weep before him to help rescue Inanna. If he doesn't care to help, then, she tells Ninshubur, go to Enki, her maternal grandfather, and weep before him. He, the god of wisdom, knows the food of life, the water of life, the secrets, so surely, she says, "He will not let me die."

Inanna begins toward the underworld but first she stops, faces Ninshubur and says, "Go now, Ninshubur. Do not forget the words I've commanded you."

Inanna proceeds and arrives at the gates of the underworld, in all her glory, dressed in the garments of her power. She knocks and demands to be let in, saying, "Open up, doorman, open up. Open up, Neti. I am all alone and I want to come in."

"Who are you?" asks Neti, the chief doorman of the underworld.

"I am Inanna, Queen of Heaven, going to the East."

"If you are going to the East, why have you travelled to the land of no return?"

"Because Gudgalanna, the Bull of Heaven, husband of my elder sister, Ereshkigal, has died; I'm here to observe his funeral rites. Let the beer of his funeral rites be poured into the cup."

The gatekeeper tells Inanna to stay put, that he must first speak to his queen before allowing her entrance. He stands before Ereshkigal and explains, "A maid as tall as heaven, as wide as the earth, as strong as the foundations of the city wall, waits outside the palace gates. She has gathered together the seven *me*, the divine powers, collected them in her hands and prepared herself..." and one by one, he recounts the seven *me* Inanna is dressed in: the crown, the wig, the beads, the mascara, the pectoral and golden ring, and the rod and measuring line.

When her sister Ereshkigal finds out that Inanna is at the gate of the underworld, dressed in her glorious ego and demanding to be let in, she's not at all happy about the news. She slaps her thigh, bites her lip, considers the situation and tells the gatekeeper to bolt the gates. She says, "Let each door of the underworld open separately, but only after Inanna has removed one article of clothing at each gate. Let her enter naked and bowed low."

Neti, the gatekeeper, following his queen's instructions, bolts the seven gates of the underworld. He opens the first gate and tells Inanna to come in. When she enters, her crown, the first of her protective *me*, is removed, depriving her of her intellect and godhood, her connection with heaven.

"What's this?" she asks.

Neti tells her to remain quiet. She must not dispute the rites of the underworld, as they are perfect.

When she enters the second gate, the lapis lazuli beads are removed from around her neck, depriving her of the power of creativity.

"What's this?" she asks.

Again, Neti tells her to remain quiet. She must not dispute the rites of the underworld, as they are perfect.

The same process continues with the next five gates, with the rest of the items being removed from her one by one as she questions why and the gatekeeper responds by telling her to remain quiet and not dispute the rites of the underworld, as they are perfect. Once the last item, the royal garment, is removed, Inanna walks naked and bowed low. Ereshkigal rises from her throne and Inanna walks toward it. The Anuna, the seven judges of the underworld, surround her and give their judgment. Ereshkigal gives her the look of death, speaks to her with anger, and pronounces over her the burden of guilt. She then turns Inanna's body into a corpse, a piece of rotting meat, and hangs the corpse on a hook.

After three days and three nights, Ninshubur sees that Inanna hasn't returned, so she carries out the instructions Inanna had given her before embarking on this journey. She laments for her, beats the drum, makes the rounds of the houses of the gods, tears at her eyes and mouth and thighs, dresses in a beggar's garment, and sets out to Nippur, the temple of Inanna's paternal grandfather Enlil. Standing before him, she cries of Inanna's trouble, how three days ago, she went to the underworld and has not returned, that he must do something to rescue her so she's not killed there.

"My daughter craved the great heaven and she craved the

great below as well," he says. "The divine powers of the underworld are divine powers which should not be craved, for whoever gets them must remain in the underworld."

Thus, he refuses to help, so Ninshubur goes to Ur, to the temple of Inanna's father, Nanna. Upon entering the temple, she cries of Inanna's trouble, how she went to the underworld and has not returned, that he must do something to rescue her so she's not killed there. Nanna responds to her basically the same way that Enlil had, and he too refuses to help. As instructed, Ninshubur travels to Eridu to the temple of Enki, Inanna's maternal grandfather. She cries of Inanna's dire situation and Enki, rather than condemn Inanna for her decision to venture to the underworld and shrug his shoulders like the others had done, actually shows concern. He asks, "What has my daughter done? The Queen of Heaven and Earth has me worried. I am troubled and grieved."

He takes action. He removes dirt from the tip of his fingernail and creates the kurgarra, a creature that's neither male nor female. He removes dirt from the tip of his other fingernail and creates galatur, a creature that's neither male nor female. To the kurgarra he gives the life-giving plant. To the galatur he gives the life-giving water. He instructs them to go to the underworld and pass through the doors like flies. He tells them that they'll find Ereshkigal crying like a woman giving birth, her breasts uncovered with no linen over her body, her hair spinning around her like leeks. She will moan and groan in agony about her insides and outsides, her belly and her back, her heart and her liver, and when she does so, the two creatures ought to mimic her words, to moan, groan and sigh with her to show compassion for her pain.

Ereshkigal will ask, "Who are you that you have this

compassion for my aches and pains? If you are gods, let me talk with you. If you are mortals, I will give you a gift." She will offer a riverful of water and a field of grains, but, Enki warns, don't accept it. Ask for the corpse of Inanna. Once she gives the corpse, sprinkle on it the life-giving plant and the life-giving water. Then Inanna will arise.

Heeding the words of Enki, the two creatures head to the underworld, slip through its gates, and enter the throne of Ereshkigal, who, just as they were told, cries of pains in her insides and outsides, her belly and back, her heart and her liver. They mimic her words and emotions and she asks them, "Who are you?" The conversation presumes just as Enki had assumed, leading the two creatures to request the corpse hanging on the hook. Ereshkigal gives it to them and they do what Enki had ordered them to do—sprinkle on the corpse the life-giving plant and the life-giving water. Inanna is revived and about to ascend from the underworld but the Annuna seize her. They say, "No one ascends from the underworld unscathed. If Inanna is to ascend from the underworld, she must provide a substitute."

Inanna agrees and the sexless beings escort Inanna up from the underworld. But a horde of angry demons follow her, demanding to take someone else down to the underworld as a replacement. These demons know no food or drink, have never enjoyed the pleasures of lovemaking or had sweet children to kiss. They're ruthless—tear away the wife from a man's embrace, snatch the child from a man's knee or a wet-nurse's breasts, make the bride leave her husband's embrace.

The band of demons enters the city with Inanna, where Ninshubur, dressed in soiled clothing, awaits behind the palace gates. Upon seeing her queen, she throws herself at her feet. The demons tell Inanna to continue into the city while they take Ninshubur to the underworld as a substitute. Inanna refuses, defends her minister with all her might by explaining how faithful and helpful she has been to her.

The demons agree to find someone else and walk on. They come upon Inanna's son, Shara, dressed in soiled clothing. He throws himself at his mother's feet. They tell Inanna to continue into the city while they take him to the underworld as a substitute. She refuses, explaining that Shara is her son who sings hymns to her, manicures her nails, and grooms her hair. She says, "I will never give Shara to you!"

The demons agree to take someone else and walk on. They come across another one of Inanna's sons, Lulal, dressed in soiled clothing. They tell her to continue into the city while they take him to the underworld as a substitute. Again she refuses, explaining that Lulal is an outstanding leader, her right arm and left arm. She says, "I will never give Lulal to you!"

They agree to take someone else and walk on. They reach the great apple tree in Uruk where Inanna discovers that her husband, Dumuzi, has not mourned her death. He's relaxing superbly on a throne, dressed in a magnificent garment, and doesn't bother to stir when Inanna returns. She's infuriated and orders the demons to take him as her replacement. The demons seize him by his thighs, pour the milk from his seven churns, and break the pipe he's playing.

Inanna gives him the look of death, speaks to him angrily, and puts the burden of guilt upon him. She demands that the demons take him to the underworld. Dumuzi lets out a wail and raises his hands to heaven, to Utu, saying, "You are my brother-in-law. I'm your relation by marriage. I brought butter to your mother's house. I brought milk to Ningal's house. I carried food to the holy shrine. I brought wedding gifts to Uruk. I danced on the holy knees, the knees of Inanna. Utu, you who are a just god, a merciful god, turn my hands into snake's hand and turn my feet into snake's feet so I can escape my demons. Let them not keep hold of me."

Utu accepts Dumuzi's tears and turns his hands into snake's hands and his feet into snake's feet. Dumuzi escapes his demons. One day, while in hiding, he has a frightening dream. He tells his little sister Geshtinanna about it, how he will be no more and the sheepfold will be given to the winds. Geshtinanna begs him not to tell her of such a dream, although she confirms that this will be his fate: the demons will pursue and attack him; his mother will tremble and mourn for him; he will be taken away first, then she, his sister.

Before Dumuzi runs off, he tells his sister and an unnamed friend not to tell anyone of his hiding place. He says, "I will hide in the grass. I will hide among the small plants. I will hide among the large plants. I will hide in the ditches of Arali."

His sister and friend respond, "Dumuzi, if we tell your hiding place, let your dogs devour us!"

Dumuzi goes into hiding and the demons search for him. They go to Geshtinanna's house and offer her the gift of water and grains to tell them where her brother is hiding. She refuses to speak so they tear her clothes and pour pitch into her vulva. Still, she doesn't speak. They leave and head to one of Dumuzi's friends. He does betray Dumuzi in exchange for the gifts the demons offer.

Once they learn of his whereabouts, the seven demons capture Dumuzi. He cries for Utu to rescue him by transforming him into a gazelle. Utu heeds his request and Dumuzi escapes, but later on, he's eventually captured while hiding in his sister's house. Each demon destroys a part of him or his belongings, the first striking his cheek with a piercing nail, another smashing the bottom of the churn, and the last one saying, "Rise, Dumuzi! Husband of Inanna, son of Sirtur, brother of Geshtinanna! Rise from your false sleep!"

He's told to remove his crown, his royalty garment and scepter, and even his sandals. They drag him naked to the underworld, and Dumuzi is no more. The sheepfold is given to the winds.

Once he's gone, Inanna has a change of heart. She weeps bitterly and continually for her young husband along with her sister-in-law and mother-in-law. The three women miss Dumuzi terribly and their grief is inconsolable. Desolation fills the land. By and by a holy fly circles about and says she'll reveal Dumuzi's place for something in return. Inanna says to the fly that, in return, she'll allow her to frequent the beer-houses and taverns, abide among conversations of the wise ones and among the songs of the musicians. The fly accepts this offer and reveals Dumuzi's place.

Inanna and Geshtinanna go there and find Dumuzi weeping. Geshtinanna volunteers to be her brother's substitute. In the end, Inanna decides that Dumuzi and his sister will each spend half the year in the underworld. She places her husband in the hands of the eternal and praises her sister Ereshkigal for her greatness and holiness.

Thus Dumuzi and Inanna are reconciled.

The story about the goddess of fertility and her mortal lover who dies for her and is resurrected is universal, appearing in mythologies and religions from many prehistoric cultures. The goddess and her lover take on different names in different cultures, but the blueprint of the story remains the same. Some anthropologists would even identify Jesus as an embodiment of the same mythical archetype manifested by Duzumi because Jesus, like Duzumi, is a young male god who dies and is resurrected.

Inanna is remembered not only in the ancient writings of Sumer. She also receives mention in the Old Testament. The people of Israel, to the great displeasure of the Jewish priesthood, are said to have baked small cakes for her festival. One website declares that Easter is not of Christian origin. It is another form of Astarte, one of the titles of the Chaldean goddess, the queen of heaven. The festival of Pasch [Passover and the Feast of Unleavens] was a continuation of the Jewish [that is, God's] feast. From this Pasch the pagan festival of Easter was quite distinct and was introduced into the apostate Western religion, as part of the attempt to adapt pagan festivals to Christianity.

According to Sue Ellen Thompson, the pagans worshiped the goddess Eostre by serving tiny cakes, often decorated with a cross, at their annual spring festival. When archaeologists excavated the city of Herculaneum in southwestern Italy, which had been buried under volcanic ash and lava since 79 CE, they found two small loaves, each with a cross on it, among the ruins.

Christians later adopted hot cross buns and repurposed the symbol of the cross, just like they did with other pagan springtime customs such as bunnies and eggs, which are tokens for fertility and birth. The cross is thought to have originally represented the phases of the moon, or the four seasons. In the Christian tradition, it now symbolizes the crucifixion and resurrection of Jesus Christ.

Inanna and Dumuzi's transformed relationship as king/queen, husband/wife, father/child, brother/sister suggests the duality of male/female, positive/negative, spirit/matter that exists throughout the cosmos. Duzumi's alternating six-month sojourns in the Great Below and six months of freedom suggests nature's seasonal changes from barrenness to abundance and, in human life, from periods of inactivity which provide time for reflection and preparation to periods of activity and expression. Sumerians believed that, while Geshtinanna was in heaven and Dumuzi in the underworld, the earth became dry and barren, causing the season of summer.

The common interpretation of this story is that Inanna gave up earthly powers and possessions to achieve wisdom and understanding. This is the initiation process into the mysteries. She went through the seven chakras, died, and returned to life with a new wisdom and understanding. Same with her husband, although he went unwillingly. The underworld was the realm under the seen, not a hell or punishment, but a spiritual realm, just another phase of existence.

Inanna embodies love and lust and in Judeo-Christian theology, love and lust are observed as completely dissimilar, one being good and the other, not so good. During Inanna's time, love and lust came together, creating a sexual act that was loving, creative, beautiful, reproductive, and healing for society. Some women today suffer from addictions and self-sabotage because of too many imbalances and unfulfilled passions.

Helen Talia once posted that Inanna represents the ever-changing human nature and the different cycles of womanhood. "We, as well, transcend from childhood to teens. We take on the roles of wives, and then become mothers (fertility). From there we learn to nurture our families, unquestionably, among the greatest gifts that a female possesses in her gift of giving (abundance). And when a woman gives, she gives of herself. In the Assyrian culture, without a doubt, motherhood is hailed as the highest role that a woman will take on in her lifetime. However, in the Western societies, the Assyrian woman has also taken on additional roles, mainly working outside her home. And while this is a highly praised socio-economic role, the Inanna in all of us, without a question, has been neglected… due to pressed schedules, competition, or our own desertion."

There are many ways to restore peace and balance within our lives, and one of the ways is doing chakra work. It is a great way to clear issues that can lead to illness as well as awaken desires within, helping us reach our highest potential and experience joy.

Eastern Etheric System
Kundalini Chakra

Crown Chakra — Spirituality
Third Eye Chakra — Awareness
Throat Chakra — Communication
Heart Chakra — Love, Healing
Solar Plexus Chakra — Wisdom, Power
Sacral Chakra — Sexuality, Creativity
Root Chakra — Basic Trust

The Eastern etheric system includes chakras, central channels, meridians, and auras. Chakra means "wheel" in Sanskrit and refers to energy generators. There are seven major chakras. They vary in color from individual to individual and will also vary within one individual from time to time. However, in a generalized way, you may find them following the color bands of the white light spectrum. In the Eastern tradition, chakras are depicted as lotus flowers in stylized two-dimensional drawings.

This is a chart from my Native American teachers' course material which introduced me to chakra work. If you've never worked with chakras before, there are many books, online videos, and local practitioners and classes that can introduce you to this practice.

First: Root Chakra—Muladhara (Root Base)
Located below the base of the spine, usually found between the knees and ankle. This chakra is sometimes referred to as the base chakra. It is associated with the physical body, survival, vitality, and the circulatory system.

Second: Sacral Chakra—Swadisthana (One's Own Abode)
Located at the genitals, it's associated with sexual energy, creativity, and relationships to others.

Third: Solar Plexus Chakra—Manipura (City of Jewels)
Located at the naval, it's associated with power, strength, courage, emotions and the digestive system.

Fourth: Heart Chakra—Anahata (the Unstruck)
Located at the base of the breast bone, it is associated with love, compassion, sensitivity, and the cardiovascular system.

Fifth: Throat Chakra—Vishuddha (Purify)
Located at the throat, it is associated with expression, will, communication, the inner voice, and clairaudience.

Sixth: Third Eye Chakra—Ajna (Command)
Located at the forehead, between the brows, this chakra is sometimes referred to as the brow chakra. It is associated with vision, perception, insight, intuition, clairvoyance, and telepathy.

Seventh: Crown Chakra—Sahasrara (Thousand Petals Lotus)
Located at the top of the head, it is associated with enlightenment, universal consciousness, oneness, and divine inspiration.

Chapter 6

Ishtar
Goddess of Fertility, Love, War, and Sex

Thirteen centuries later, around 2000-1600 BC, Inanna becomes identified by the Akkadians and Babylonians as the goddess Ishtar, and further down the line, the biblical Ashtoreth, the Phoenician Astarte, the Greek Aphrodite, among many others. Her Babylonian legends diverge from the earlier Sumerian

Mesopotamian Goddesses

tales. *Inanna's Descent to the Underworld*, for instance, is a poem that contains 415 lines and, by contrast, the Babylonian Ishtar's Descent is told in 145 lines. It's suggested that the difference is due to the influence of patriarchy, which diminishes the power and importance of this goddess during the second millennium BC. This is clearly seen in the Babylonian *Epic of Gilgamesh*, the oldest epic tale in the world which was written in the second millennium BC 1500 years before Homer, in cuneiform on 123 clay tablets, and which was discovered in Nineveh by Hormuzd Rassam in 1853.

Gilgamesh, the son of goddess Ninsun and the priest-king Lugalbanda, is two-thirds god and one-third man. He's handsome, energetic, and mighty, but he's also cruel and arrogant. During his reign as king of Uruk, he builds splendid ziggurats and surrounds his city with high walls. He gives himself the right to lord over his people by combating the young men and demanding to be the first to sleep with the brides on their wedding night.

The people plead for the gods to rescue them from Gilgamesh's tyranny, crying, "Gilgamesh sounds the tocsin for his amusement; his arrogance has no bounds by day or night. No son is left with his father, for Gilgamesh takes them all, even the children; yet the king should be a shepherd to his people. His lust leaves no virgin to her lover, neither the warrior's daughter nor the wife of the noble; yet this is the shepherd of the city, wise, comely and resolute."

The gods decide to create a man equal in strength that could stop Gilgamesh's tyranny and arrogance. Aruru, the goddess of creation, uses clay and water to make Enkidu, a wild man raised by animals and oblivious of human society. He had a rough body and long hair like a woman. He eats grass in the hills with the gazelle and lurks with the wild beasts at the water-holes. He fills the pits that the trapper digs and tears up the traps so he can help the beasts escape.

One day, Enkidu comes across the trapper who, upon seeing him, is frozen with fear. The trapper returns to his house and tells his father what he has seen, describing Enkidu as "The strongest in the world, like an immortal from heaven." His father suggests that the trapper goes to the city, praise to Gilgamesh the wild man's strength and distinctiveness, and ask for a woman from the temple of love who would use her woman's art to tame Enkidu into a civilized man so that he's no longer able to live with the wild beasts as they, once he's touched by a human, will then reject him. Gilgamesh agrees to this plan and tells the trapper to take a woman from the temple of love.

The trapper brings Shamhat to the drinking hole where the wild animals come to drink water. When she sees Enkidu, she removes her clothes, stands naked before him, and teaches him the art of lovemaking. They spend six days and seven nights together, and afterward, Enkidu returns to the wilderness where the animals, picking up the scent of his transformation, flee from him. He wants to follow but his body feels weak, for wisdom has entered him and the thoughts of men are now in his heart. So he returns and sits down at Shamhat's feet and listens keenly to what she tells him.

"You are wise, Enkidu, and now you have become like a god," she says. "Why do you want to run wild with the beasts in the hills? Come with me. I will take you to strong-walled Uruk, to the blessed temple of Ishtar and Anu, of love and of heaven. There Gilgamesh lives, who is very strong, and like a wild bull he lords it over men."

Enkidu is pleased, feels he has a new purpose in life, and

agrees to go along with her to Uruk. He says he'll challenge Gilgamesh boldly and change the old order. She says she'll take him there, where he'll stand before Gilgamesh, but advises him the following: "Leave your boasting. Gilgamesh is stronger than you. Shamash the glorious sun has given favors to him, and Anu of the heavens, and Enlil, and Ea the wise has given him deep understanding. I tell you, even before you have left the wilderness, Gilgamesh will know in his dreams that you are coming."

Shamhat tears her clothing in two, places one piece of the clothing around him and the other around her. She leads him to the sheepfold where the shepherds serve bread and wine. He eats, drinks, and becomes merry. He combs his hair, anoints himself with oil, and looks like a bridegroom. He helps the men hunt lions and catch wolves and lives happily among them until, one day, he sees a man approaching.

The man says, "Gilgamesh has gone into the marriage house and shut out the people. He does strange things in Uruk, the city of great streets. At the roll of the drum work begins for the men and work for the women. Gilgamesh the king is about to celebrate marriage with the Queen of Love, and he still demands to be first with the bride, the king to be first and the husband to follow, for that was ordained by the gods from his birth, from the time the umbilical cord was cut. But now the drums roll for the choice of the bride and the city groans."

Enkidu says that he will go to Gilgamesh, challenge him boldly, and change the old order. When he enters Uruk, behind him Shamhat and behind her the man, people in the market are in awe over his resemblance to Gilgamesh and they rejoice that Gilgamesh has now met his match. Meanwhile, the bridal bed is made and the bride waits for the bridegroom. At night, Gilgamesh comes to the house but Enkidu blocks the way at the gate. He puts his foot in front of Gilgamesh to prevent him from entering. The two grapple, holding each other like bulls, and get into a big brawl that causes the shattering of doorposts and the shaking of the walls. When Gilgamesh throws Enkidu, Enkidu praises his strength, saying, among many things, "Your strength surpasses the strength of men."

With this, the men embrace and their friendship is sealed. They become inseparable like brothers. Later on, Gilgamesh desires to gain more power. He wants his name to be stamped on bricks next to the names of famous men and proposes to go to the forest to destroy Humbaba, whose name means hugeness and who Gilgamesh calls evil even though Humbaba hasn't done anything harmful to his people. Enlil had appointed Humbaba to guard the forest, the tens of thousands of cedar trees, and Humbaba was merely minding his own business.

Enkidu objects to this idea, since he'd lived in the wild and was friends with nature, including Humbaba. He explains to Gilgamesh that the forest is the sacred realm of the gods and not meant for mortals, but Gilgamesh tantalizes him, saying, "How is it, already you are afraid! I will go first although I am your lord and you may safely call out, 'Forward, there is nothing to fear!' Then if I fall I leave behind me a name that endures."

Enkidu and the council of elders of Uruk try to deter Gilgamesh from his plan to kill Humbaba, but to no avail. His mother also complains of his restless ways, but ultimately gives in. She prays for the sun god Shamash to give her son support, and adopting Enkidu as her second son, she places an amulet for a pledge around his neck and says to him, "I entrust my son to you; bring him back to me safely."

Armed with weapons for the battle, the men begin their long journey toward the forest. At one point, Enkidu stops and tells Gilgamesh that they shouldn't go. Gilgamesh tells him not to be a coward, adding, "Forget death and follow me, a man resolute in action, but one who is not foolhardy. When two go together each will protect himself and shield his companion, and if they fall they leave an enduring name."

They continue on their journey and then, a second time, Enkidu attempts to persuade Gilgamesh to leave this plan behind and return home. Gilgamesh refuses, saying, "If your heart is fearful throw away fear; if there is terror in it throw away terror. Take your axe in your hand and attack. He who leaves the fight unfinished is not at peace."

They arrive to Humbaba's strong house of cedar. When Humbaba comes out, Enkidu urges for Gilgamesh to quickly attack him. Humbaba threatens Gilgamesh with cries and the eye of death while Gilgamesh prays for Shamash to help him. Shamash summons the great wind to cripple Humbaba. Humbaba turns pale and with tears in his eyes begs Gilgamesh to spare his life. He promises to be Gilgamesh's servant, to give him all the trees, to cut them down and build him a palace. He takes his hand and takes him to his house so that the heart of Gilgamesh is moved with compassion. But Enkidu says this will never be so!

Humbaba says, "Enkidu, what you have spoken is evil; you, a hireling, dependent for your bread! In envy and for fear of a rival you have spoken evil words."

"Do not listen, Gilgamesh," Enkidu responds. "This Humbaba must die. Kill Humbaba first and his servants after."

Gilgamesh strikes Humbaba with a thrust of the sword to the neck, and Enkidu strikes the second blow. At the third blow Humbaba falls. They then attack the cedars, with Gilgamesh cutting the trees and Enkidu clearing their roots as far as the banks of the Euphrates. They uncover the sacred dwellings of the Anunnaki, kiss the ground and set Humbaba's head before the gods, before Enlil, boastful of their wicked ways and hungry for immortality.

Enlil, enraged that they'd defied the gods, asks, "Why did you do this thing? From henceforth may the fire be on your faces, may it eat the bread that you eat, may it drink where you drink."

Still drunk with pride over his victory, Gilgamesh is not concerned with these words. He washes his long locks and cleans his weapons from the blood of Humbaba, removes his stained clothes, then wears his royal robes and crown. When Ishtar sees him, she says, "Come to me Gilgamesh, and be my bridegroom; grant me seed of your body, let me be your bride and you shall be my husband."

She offers him all sorts of enticements, such as power and a chariot of lapis lazuli and of gold, with wheels of gold and horns of copper. He says to glorious Ishtar, "If I take you in marriage, what gifts can I give in return?" He counts some of the gifts he could give, bread and wine fit for gods and queens, enough barley to stuff her warehouse, but making her his wife, "That I will not. How would it go with me? Your lovers have found you like a brazier which smolders in the cold, a backdoor which keeps out neither squall of wind nor storm..." He goes on and on with insults, and asks, "Which of your lovers did you ever love forever? What shepherd of yours has pleased you for all time? Listen to me while I tell the tale of your lovers."

One by one, he recounts their stories.

"There was Tammuz (Dumuzi), the lover of your youth, for him you decreed wailing, year after year. You loved the many colored roller, but still you struck and broke his wing;

now in the grove he sits and cries, 'Kappi, kappi, my wing, my wing.' You have loved the lion tremendous in strength: seven pits you dug for him. You have loved the stallion magnificent in battle, and for him you decreed whip and spur and a thong, to gallop seven leagues by force and to muddy the water before he drinks; and for his mother Silili lamentations. You have loved the shepherd of the flock; he made meal-cake for you day after day, he killed kids for your sake. You struck and turned him into a wolf. Now his own herd-boys chase him away, his own hounds worry his flanks. And did you not love Ishullanu, the gardener of your father's palm grove? He brought you baskets filled with dates without end: every day he loaded your table. Then you turned your eyes on him and said, 'Dearest Ishullanu, come here to me, let us enjoy your manhood, come forward and take me, I am yours.' Ishullanu answered, 'What are you asking from me? My mother has baked and I have eaten; why should I come to such as you for food that is tainted and rotten? For when was a screen of rushes sufficient protection from frosts?' But when you had heard his answer you struck him. He was changed to a blind mole deep in the earth, one whose desire is always beyond his reach. And if you and I should be lovers, should not I be served in the same fashion as all these others whom you loved once?"

Ishtar is offended and insists that her father send the Bull of Heaven to make Gilgamesh pay a price for his rejection, threatening to raise the dead if he doesn't. Her mother warns that the Bull of Heaven will bring along seven years of drought throughout Uruk. Ishtar assures her that she has saved enough grain for the people and grass for the cattle. So the Bull of Heaven is sent from heaven, bringing with it a great drought and plague of the land, but Gilgamesh and Enkidu slay the beast and offer its heart to Shamash. Enkidu throws the bull's hindquarters at Ishtar's face and says, "If I could lay my hands on you, it is this I should do to you, and drape his innards over your arms."

Ishtar calls together her people, the dancing and singing girls, the sacred lovers of the temple, and laments over the thigh of the Bull of Heaven. Gilgamesh, proud of the Bull's horns, which weigh thirty pounds each, carries them into the palace and hangs them on the wall. Then he and his friend drive through the streets of Uruk, with Gilgamesh asking the singing girls, "Who is most glorious of the heroes, who is most eminent among men?" and they answering, "Gilgamesh is the most glorious of heroes, Gilgamesh is the most eminent among men." A grand celebration ensues in the palace.

In the morning, Enkidu tells Gilgamesh that he has had a bad dream where the gods took council and decided that one of them must die for killing the Bull of Heaven and Humbaba, who guarded the cedar forests. His dream becomes a reality. The gods decide to kill Enkidu as punishment, so Enkidu falls ill. As he lies on his deathbed, he pours his heart to Gilgamesh. "It was I who cut down the cedar, I who leveled the forest, I who slew Humbaba and now see what has become of me."

When Enkidu descends to the underworld, Gilgamesh is devastated. He refuses to leave his side or permit his corpse to be buried until six days and seven nights after his death, when maggots begin to fall from his body. Gilgamesh cannot rest. Afraid of death and determined to avoid Enkidu's fate, he journeys into the wilderness to visit Utnapishtim and his wife, the only humans to have survived the Great Flood and who were granted immortality by the gods. They live in another world called Dilmun, the garden of the gods. From them, he wants to discover the secret of everlasting life.

Gilgamesh crosses great rivers and oceans and mountains; he tackles and slays monstrous mountain lions, bears and other beasts. Along the way, he meets Siduri, a tavern keeper at the beach beside the sea of the dead, who discourages him from the journey. She says, "Gilgamesh, where are you going? The life you seek you shall never find. When the gods created humankind, death they appointed for humans. Life in their own hands they retained. Gilgamesh, let your belly be full. Enjoy yourself day and night. Every day make merry, dance, and play. Let your clothes be clean. Let your head be washed. Bathe yourself in water. Gaze upon the little child that holds your hand. Let a wife enjoy your repeated embrace. For this is the lot of men."

But Gilgamesh is not satisfied with earthly pleasures. He's determined to continue his search for immortality. When he finally reaches the island of Dilmun, Utnapishtim tells him something similar to what Siduri had said. "There is no permanence. Do we build a house to stand forever? Do we seal a contract to hold for all time? From the days of old there is no permanence. The sleeping and the dead, how alike they are, they are like a painted death. What is there between the master and the servant when both have fulfilled their doom? When the Anunnaki, the judges, and Mammetun, the mother of destinies, come together they decree the fates of men. Life and death they allot but the day of death they do not disclose."

Gilgamesh insists that Utnapishtim reveal to him the mystery of everlasting life, so Utnapishtim tells him the story of how he survived the Great Flood. The flood was brought to the world by the god Enlil who wanted to destroy all of mankind for the noise, confusion, and babel they had brought to the world. His half-brother, the god Enki, also known as Ea, warned Utnapishtim of this flood and told him to build a ship and load it with his treasures, his family, and the seeds of all living things. The rains came as promised, covering the world with water and killing everything except Utnapishtim and his boat. The boat docked on the tip of Nisir Mountain, where Utnapishtim and his family waited for the waters to subside.

On the seventh day Utnapishtim released a dove. She flew away but finding no resting-place, she returned. Then he released a swallow, and she did the same as the dove. When he released a raven, she saw that the waters had retreated. She ate, flew around, cawed, and returned to Utnapishtim. Utnapishtim made sacrifices and libations to the gods, and the gods, smelling the sweet savor, gathered like flies over the sacrifice. Ishtar also attended. She removed her necklace with the jewels of heaven that once Anu had made to please her and said, "O you gods here present, by the lapis lazuli round my neck I shall remember these days as I remember the jewels of my throat; these last days I shall not forget. Let all the gods gather round the sacrifice, except Enlil. He shall not approach this offering, for without reflection he brought the flood; he consigned my people to destruction."

When Enlil learned there were survivors from the flood, he became angry. Enki intervened and counseled him to make his peace with Utnapishtim and his wife. Eventually Enki did bless them and granted them everlasting life. He then took them to live in the land of the gods on the island of Dilmun. This experience made Enlil realize that humans are indispensible to the gods. He therefore promised that he will not attempt to eliminate mankind again if humans practiced birth control and lived in harmony with the natural world.

After sharing this story, Utnapishtim offers Gilgamesh a

chance for immortality by putting him through a test; he must stay awake for six days and seven nights. Before Utnapishtim finishes explaining the test, Gilgamesh has fallen asleep, exhausted from his journey.

Utnapishtim says to his wife, "Look at him now, the strong man who would have everlasting life. Even now the mists of sleep are drifting over him."

His wife says to wake him up so that he can return to his land in peace, but Utnapishtim says, "All men are deceivers. Even you he will attempt to deceive." He instructs her to bake loaves of bread, each day one loaf, and put it beside his head and make a mark on the wall to number the days that he slept. There came a day when the first loaf was hard, the second like leather, the third soggy, the crust of the fourth had mold, the fifth was mildewed, the sixth fresh and the seventh still on the embers. Then Utnapishtim touched Gilgamesh and he awoke.

"I hardly slept when you touched and roused me," says Gilgamesh.

"Count these loaves and learn how many days you slept," says Utnapishtim.

Gilgamesh realizes he failed the test and prepares for departure.

After he bathed in the washing area and dressed in clean and new garments, he and his ferryman board the boat. They're ready to sail away when the wife of Utnapishtim suggests that they give him a gift to take home since he has wearied himself out coming to Dilmun. Utnapishtim says that there's a plant that grows under the water. It has a prickle like the thorn on a rose and will wound the hands. But if one succeeds in taking it, it will restore the person to their youth.

Gilgamesh is happily able to capture the marvelous plant

and even gives it the name "The Old Men are Young Again," with the plan of sharing it with the old men in Uruk. He and his ferryman leave Dilmun and head to Uruk. Once when they stop for the night, while Gilgamesh bathes in a well of cool water, a serpent steals the plant and slithers away, shedding its skin and becoming young again. Once again, as he had with the pukku and mikku that Inanna fashioned for him in the earlier story *The Huluppu-Tree*, Gilgamesh loses the gifts he has been given. Gilgamesh is in tears, crying to his ferryman that he has toiled in vain. "For myself I have gained nothing; not I, but the beast of the earth has joy of it [the plant] now."

Having lost both opportunities to gain immortality, he returns empty-handed to his city of Uruk, where he reconciles with his mortality, and in time, he too dies.

Mesopotamian Goddesses

The Epic of Gilgamesh, which predates genesis by far, is a collection of stories handed down orally until various unknown authors began to write it down. The first modern translation of the Epic was published in the early 1870s by George Smith who then made further discoveries on his later expeditions. Smith gave the final translation in his book *The Chaldean Account of Genesis* in 1876.

Based on the brutally negative depiction of Ishtar in this tablet, scholars have reasoned that Gilgamesh's rejection of Ishtar reveals a deeper scheme. He's rejecting goddess worship in favor of patriarchy. Enkidu's behavior toward her is even worse. They forget they are mortals and take the liberty to treat Ishtar with enjoyable contempt at a time when it was required that the king become the sexual consort of the high priestess, incarnation of the goddess on earth, who held the rights to the royal throne through matrilineal descent. The goddess is offended by their behavior, and some say, by Gilgamesh's love for a companion of his own gender, whether chaste or unchaste.

Merlin Stone notes that Ishtar was revered as "majestic queen whose decrees are preeminent." In one text Ishtar Herself says, "When at a trial of judgment I am present, a woman understanding the matter, I am." At Nimrud, in northern Mesopotamia, records of female judges and magistrates have been unearthed, testifying to the vital and respected position women held there even in the eighth century BC. In several cities there were accounts of Babylonian priestesses who acted as oracular prophetesses, providing military and political advice to kings and leaders, revealing their powerful influence upon the affairs of state. Accounts of women scribes occur in all Babylonian periods, though there were more males in this field than women.

Stone adds that laws changed later in Babylonia. Women couldn't engage in business unless it was directed by her husband, son, or brother-in-law. If anyone engaged in business with her, even if he insisted that he didn't know she was married, he was to be prosecuted as a criminal. Over time, permanent hereditary kingship became the rule and as the male deity gained supremacy, the role of the benefactor of the divine right to the throne was eventually shifted over to him, a concept of the rights of royalty that survives even today.

Ishtar would be revered in Babylon until the region was conquered by Muslims in the seventh century AD. Inanna/Ishtar, in other words, ruled the heavens for at least 2,800 years in Mesopotamia, and she has been absent from the throne for only 1,300—less than half the length of her rule. Visitors to the city of Babylon went through the magnificent lapis lazuli and golden Ishtar Gate built by Nebuchadnezzar II, which had a place for a time on the list of the Seven Wonders of the Ancient World. She still reigns in the spring celebration of Easter.

Back to Gilgamesh, whose thirst for power and immortality seems to have set the foundation for a dictatorship-ruled region. He first slays nature, the very thing that sustains us, through Humbaba, the lord of the forest. Even though Humbaba has done no harm, Gilgamesh calls him evil. Later, when Gilgamesh has finished destroying Humbaba and the forest, he shames Ishtar, a goddess, for wanting to be his wife. He points out her past lovers and accuses her of malice. He fears her intention when perhaps all she wants to do is subdue his rage through love in order to save society from further damage.

Sexually active women were made to feel shame. Since the Levite Laws of the Israelites, from Moses onward, society has demanded that women must remain a virgin until marriage or else be put to death by stoning or burning. Unfaithful married women endured the same fate. None of the laws, however, applied to men. In the worship of the female deity, sex was Her gift to humanity. It was sacred and holy. She was the Goddess of Sexual Love and Procreation. But in the religions of today we find an almost totally reversed attitude. Sex, especially non-marital sex, is considered to be naughty, dirty, even sinful. Yet rather than calling the earliest religions, which embraced such an open acceptance of all human sexuality, "fertility-cults," we might consider the religions of today as strange in that they seem to associate shame and even sin with the very process of conceiving new human life. Perhaps centuries from now scholars and historians will be classifying them as "sterility-cults."

Evidence from Sumer, Babylon, Canaan, Anatolia, Cyprus, Greece and even the Bible reveals that, despite the fact that the concept of marriage was known in the earliest written records, married women, as well as single women, continued to live for periods of time within the temple complex and to follow the ancient sexual customs of the goddess. The Bible itself reveals that these women were free to come and go as they pleased.

Women of wealthy and royal families, as well as women of the community, participated in the sexual customs of the goddess. These women were free to marry at any time and even as late as the first century BC they were considered to be exceptionally good wives. In earliest historic times, never was the question or even the concept of respectability or propriety raised—it was later invented as the new morality.

Historically, women who showed anger or acted aggressively were stereotyped as unfeminine, looked at as villains, and even considered crazy. Rather than being asked why they behaved the way they did, they were demonized. When men get angry, their power grows. The truth is that getting angry is a great teacher. Everyone feels anger, so it's normal. People simply need to take care of that anger right away, constructively, and not let it simmer and stew in their hearts. Releasing it constructively can help transform us so that we don't use the anger to hurt ourselves or others.

Over the ages, many women have had to find ways to remain silent and suppress experiences that even religions and society deem wrong. For instance, sexual assault, which is not about sexuality alone but the power to possess. Sadhguru says that one fundamental mistake that society has made is that somewhere in the minds of the male youths, we've implanted, consciously or subconsciously, that a female is an object, a commodity which doesn't have a mind of its own so that a father can "give her away."

It took the twenty-first century and a Me Too Movement

for women all over the world to feel liberated to unleash years of pent-up anger and frustration and to show the world that sexual harassment is inappropriate and harmful behavior that has been either minimized or swept under the rug. The movement brought revelations to many men and women. Men realized that almost all girls/women have in their lifetime been, at the very least, touched inappropriately by an adult male.

In many cases, a girl's first sexual experience stemmed from sexual assault or harassment. Whether she lived in Baghdad, Paris, Hong Kong or Detroit, some man, or maybe men, regarded her as a sexual object, even when she was a child. Women, including myself, took for granted the impropriety of this behavior and how abnormal it was that we and our female relatives and friends had endured this, shrugging it off with the attitude that "boys will be boys."

But we must be careful. The Me Too Movement ought not to be used as a way to condemn men or exalt women or create a divide among the genders. We already have enough of that, which unfortunately, has confused many women and led them down the wrong path. The movement ought not strangle purity, innocence, and playfulness by doing what a Cleveland radio station recently did, which is ban the classic Christmas song "Baby, It's Cold Outside" because of its lyrics. If we refuse to do the work on ourselves and insist on blaming our partner for our ineptitudes, we will just end up in a similar situation with a different man. The body changes but not the lesson. The lesson will chase us until we learn it, even if that means all the way to our grave.

Sadhguru said that if we want a better society and not just better laws, we have to create a more stable life for our youths. We need to find profound thought-out solutions and not simply react with one violent act against another violent act. The world will not change with stricter laws and more protests, he said, but with individual transformation. A transformed person lives in a cultivated way not because they fear the law, but because they have magnificent ideas about themselves that go beyond their physical nature. Each time a person transforms, they then can help someone else transform, and so on. Then violence would go down considerably.

The Me Too Movement is an opportunity to educate and communicate, for men and women to take further responsibility for their words and actions and then enjoy a healthier and higher interaction with one another. The easiest thing to do in such situations is give your power away by becoming a victim. Women's deep wounds have caused them to be trapped in victimhood. There, it's difficult to take responsibility for one's life. For most people, it's easier to blame others for their mishaps.

Forgiving and letting go, building confidence, and shifting thoughts from that of a victim to survivor are not easy to do for women. But it's a must because the truth is that you are only the reflection of your own thoughts and should not blame anyone for your life. Often, people don't look within until their life reaches the darkest point, but that's when you can learn many valuable lessons. Then, by taking the right action at the right time, your life can be transformed.

If we categorize women as good and men as bad, we deny ourselves the pleasure of a beautiful union. If we go too far with this movement, taking everything out of context, interpreting all flirtatious signals as harassment, then we will not know what it's like to meet our mate at an equal level and will never enjoy a respectful intimacy.

According to George Ohsawa, "Societies of the Far East

are feminist despite all outward appearances to the contrary... They are based on the biological and physiological superiority of women. The mother is the creator; the father is the destroyer. Man is the warrior, woman the peacemaker."

He continues to say that the United States is a great society which extolls human freedom above all else and yet four out of five people long pitifully for sexual freedom and experience misery in their marital lives. Hardly one man out of a thousand seems to find continuing joy and happiness in married life. So many people cannot enjoy sexual love and they spend their lives constantly searching for new kinds of compensatory sensory pleasure.

Ohsawa believes that "Most of the unhappiness and misery in family life stems from sexual difficulties—impotence, lack of a joyous sex life, or its opposite—too much pathological sexual activity between the spouses. No one can be truly happy unless his sexual needs are joyously satisfied in his family life. Many a great man has come to a tragic end because his wife was unbalanced sexually. What is the root cause of this continuing warfare between frigid women and tired, listless men, lacking zest for the joyous consummation of their normal sexual desires? Normal, moderate and natural sexual desire is a sign of good health."

Ohsawa says that the imbalances of yin and yang, whether in men or women, are what's violating natural laws and pushing us toward misery. How does this relate to Ishtar and Gilgamesh? Ishtar was reaching out to Gilgamesh, offering sensual love, and he was repulsed. He turned an act of love with a powerful, confident, and feminine woman into something reckless and devilish. He treated her gesture with disdain, disrespected her, and made many accusations which upset her perhaps because they were untrue. He then went out of his way to find loftier things in life that were absent of love and women. He wanted immortality. Gilgamesh was too yang, action and ego-oriented, and too much yang, Ohsawa writes, causes an abnormality that leads to great unhappiness. Too much yin, passivity, causes a man or woman to not stand up for themselves and be easily taken advantage of.

If you want love and a lasting relationship, you must regularly balance your feminine and masculine energies. Women and men are both important and, as with everything else, were created different for a reason. They are meant to be partners, friends, lovers, parents, and co-workers for the benefit of humanity.

Chapter 7

Ninlil
Lady of the Wind

The prosperous and well-developed city of Nibru, or Nippur, has a holy river called Idsala, along with wells, canals, river quays, and much cultivated land. In this urban center of the gods, which is governed by divine law, lives a young man named Enlil, the lord of the wind, and a young woman named Sud. Her name changes to Ninlil after she marries Enlil.

Sud is the daughter of Haia, the god of the stores, and Nisaba, the goddess of grain and writing. Nisaba is the chief scribe of Nanshe, and on the first day of the new year, she and Nanshe work together to settle disputes between mortals and give aid to those in need. She keeps a record of visitors seeking aid and then arranges them into a line to stand before her sister Nanshe, goddess of social justice and divination. She's also a caretaker for Ninhursag's temple at Kesh, where she gives commands and keeps temple records.

Nisaba, the old wise woman, has raised her daughter Sud to be full of flourishing beauty. She tells Sud, the object of admiration and a virgin, not to bathe in the holy river or along the canal bank, warning her that, "Enlil, the Great Mountain, will look at you. His eye is sharp. He will want to have sex with you. He will want to kiss. He will be happy to pour semen into your womb, and once done, he will simply leave you!"

Sud listens to her mother's advice but does not obey. She bathes in the river and walks along the canal bank. As her mother had predicted, Enlil notices her. He has never been married, and he has traveled through Sumer and to the end of the universe, in search throughout the land for a wife. When he sets his bright eyes on Sud, he's enthralled by her beauty. It's love at first sight. He says, "I want to have sex with you. I want to kiss you."

The feelings are not mutual. Sud refuses his advances, and he persists. She continues to refuse, telling him, "My vulva is small. It does not know pregnancy. My lips are young. They do not know kissing. If my mother learns of it, she'll slap my hand. If my father learns of it, he will grab me harshly. But no one can stop me from telling this to my girlfriend."

Sud uses this excuse to run and tell her friends. After she

leaves, Enlil summons his minister Nuska and asks him, "Has anyone made love or kissed this beautiful and radiant young woman?"

Nuska understands what his master wants and helps bring him across the river by a boat. When he sees Sud, Enlil gets out of the boat, grabs hold of her, and lies with her on a small bank where they kiss and make love. At that moment, Nanna, the moon god, is conceived. Then Enlil, who doesn't yet have a wife, asks Sud to marry him, saying, "I will make you perfect in a queen's dress. How impressed I am by your beauty, even if you are a shameless person!"

She repudiates him for suggesting or mistaking her for a loose girl and says, "If I want to stand proudly at our gate, who dares to give me a bad reputation? What are your intentions? Why have you come here? Get out of my sight!"

Standing closer to her, Enlil says, "Come, I want to speak to you, to have a talk with you about becoming my wife. Kiss me, my lady of most beautiful eyes. The matter rests in your hands."

He has barely completed his sentence when she goes into her house and closes the door.

His heart pounding, he summons Nuska and tells him to quickly go to Uruk, the city of Nisaba, and send her a message that he wants her daughter's hand in marriage. He instructs him to repeat these exact words: "I am a young man. I have sent this message to you because of my wish. I want to take your daughter as a wife. Give me your consent. I will send you presents in my name as marriage gifts. I am Enlil, the descendant and offspring of Ancar (Anu), the noble, the lord of heaven and earth. The name of your daughter shall become Ninlil, and all the foreign countries shall know it. I will present her with the

Jajiccua as her storehouse and will give the Kiur as her beloved private quarters. She shall live with me in the Ekur, my august dais. She shall determine fates. She shall apportion the divine powers among the Anunnaki, the great gods. As for you, I will place in your hands the lives of the black-headed people."

Enlil sends Nuska quickly on his way, with some jewelry in his left hand. Nuska wastes no time going to Uruk. He enters the residence of Nisaba and prostrates himself before her on her dais. He delivers Enlil's message, to which Nisaba says, "Adviser, fit for his king, ever observant! Who like you could give counsel daily to the Great Mountain? How could I contest the king's message which his slave has received? If there is truth in what you have told me—and may there be no falsehood—who could reject one who bestows such exceedingly great favors? This makes our mood and hearts happy. Let us consider that amends have been made. By bringing the marriage gifts and the presents in his name, the insult is wiped away. Tell Enlil, 'You shall become my son-in-law; do as you wish!' Let his sister come from her side, and he shall accompany Sud from here. Aruru shall become Sud's sister-in-law: let her be shown the household. Inform your lord of this. Repeat it to him in the privacy of his holy chamber."

She then goes to her daughter Sud and tells her to wash the hands of Nuska, the knowing and wise, and to pour him beer. Sud follows her mother's instructions and the minister opens his left hand and gives her the jewelry. He sets all the gifts before her, and afterward, he returns to Nibru. Nuska kisses the ground before Enlil and tells him what Nisaba, the great lady, had said. He repeats her every word, which makes Enlil rejoice.

Enlil gathers the gifts and sets out to Uruk. He raises his head, signaling for the animals to come running. Wild bulls, red deer, elephants, fallow deer, bears, wild sheep, rams, foxes, wild cats and tigers, water buffaloes, monkeys, cows and their calves, wild cattle with wide spread horns, pushed together noisily. Enlil dispatches them toward Uruk along with large and small cheeses, mustard-flavored cheeses, milk, cold hard-boiled eggs, butter, and the sweetest dry honey and white honey. He also dispatches to Uruk baskets of figs, palm dates, large pomegranates, nuts, almonds, acorns, large pomegranate seeds squeezed out from their rinds, big clusters of early grapes, trees and fruits from the orchards. And he dispatches to Uruk rock-crystal, gold, silver. The heavy loads of gifts, as they're transported, cause the dust to rise high to the sky like rain clouds. Enormous wedding gifts are brought to Nisaba, filling the city of Uruk inside and out.

Nuska treats Nisaba kindly, but she ignores his flattery and speaks to her daughter, saying, "May you be the wife of Enlil's heart, and may he speak to you sweetly. May he embrace you, the most beautiful of all, and tell you, 'Beloved, open wide!' May the two of you never lose the pleasure of excitement; make it last a long time. May you have children afterward! When you enter the house to live there, may abundance precede you, and may joy follow you. May the people line up for you wherever you go. The fate I have determined for you should be fulfilled, cannot be altered. Go with head held high into Ec-mah."

Then Aruru grasped Sud's hand and led her away into the Ec-mah. She brought her into the E-kur, the house of Enlil, where in the sleeping quarters was a flowered bed fragrant like cedar forests. There, Enlil made love to his wife and took great pleasure in it. He says, "From now on, a foreign woman shall be the mistress of the house. May my beautiful wife, who was born by holy Nisaba, be Ninlil, the growing grain, the life of

Sumer. When you appear in the furrows like a beautiful young girl, may Ickur, the canal inspector, be your provider, supplying you with water from the ground. The height of the year is marked with your new prime flax and your new prime grain; Enlil and Ninlil procreate them as desired."

Everything is nice and dandy until one day, Enlil is walking in the city, and for unclear reasons, he's confronted and placed under arrest by the authority of his fellow gods. They shout at him, "Enlil, you are ritually impure. Get out of the city. We do not want people like you here."

In accordance with the gods' demands, Enlil leaves the city. Ninlil follows him. Wanting to continue to have a relationship with his wife and create more offspring, he comes up with an idea. He tells the gatekeeper, "If you should see Ninlil pass by, and if she should ask for me, don't tell her where I am."

Enlil then disguises himself as the gatekeeper and, when shortly afterward, Ninlil comes passing by, she asks him, "Have you seen your lord Enlil? When did he go by?"

"My lord Enlil has not talked to me, lovely one," the gatekeeper replies.

"I will make clear my aim and explain my intent. You can fill my womb once it is empty. Enlil, lord of all the lands, has had sex with me! Just as Enlil is your lord, so am I your lady!"

"If you are my lady, let my hand touch your intimate parts."

"The seed of your lord, the bright seed, is in my womb."

"My master's seed can go up to the heavens! Let my seed go downwards instead of my master's seed!"

Ninlil sees a resemblance to Enlil in this city gatekeeper, so she agrees. They lay down and he makes love to her, kisses her there, from whom Nergal is conceived, he who would control access to the underworld and for a time be a gatekeeper at one of its gates. Then Enlil goes along and Ninlil follows. He approaches the man of Id-kura, river of the underworld, and instructs him, "When your lady Ninlil comes, if she asks of my whereabouts, don't tell her where I am!"

Enlil then disguises himself as the man of Id-kura, the man-eating river. Shortly afterward, Ninlil comes passing by, and she asks him, "Have you seen your lord Enlil? When did he go by?"

"My lord Enlil has not talked to me, lovely one," he says.

"I will make clear my aim and explain my intent. You can fill my womb once it is empty. Enlil, lord of all the lands, has had sex with me! Just as Enlil is your lord, so am I your lady!"

"If you are my lady, let my hand touch your intimate parts."

"The seed of your lord, the bright seed, is in my womb."

"My master's seed can go up to the heavens! Let my seed go downwards instead of my master's seed!"

Ninlil sees a resemblance to Enlil in this Id-kura, the man-eating river. They lay down and he makes love to her, kisses her there, from which Ninazu is conceived, the king who stretches measuring lines over the fields. Then Enlil goes along and Ninlil follows. He approaches the man of the ferryboat and instructs him, "When your lady Ninlil comes, if she asks of my whereabouts, don't tell her where I am."

Enlil disguises himself as the man of the ferryboat. Shortly afterward, Ninlil comes passing by, and she asks him, "Have you seen your lord Enlil? When did he go by?"

"My lord Enlil has not talked to me, lovely one," he says.

"I will make clear my aim and explain my intent. You can fill my womb once it is empty. Enlil, lord of all the lands, has had sex with me! Just as Enlil is your lord, so am I your lady!"

"If you are my lady, let my hand touch your intimate parts."

"The seed of your lord, the bright seed, is in my womb."

"My master's seed can go up to the heavens! Let my seed go downwards instead of my master's seed!"

Ninlil sees a resemblance to Enlil in this ferryboat man. They lay down and he makes love to her, kisses her there, from which Enbilulu is conceived, the inspector of canals. And so four sons are born to Ninlil, and ever after, she would speak the praises of Enlil and Enlil would return them. The couple in union administer the *me*, which they brought forth together, conferring the highest privileges upon their granddaughter goddess Inanna and decreeing the fates of gods and men.

After Enlil forces himself onto Ninlil, she defends her rights by turning him over to the assembly of Anunnaki gods, which he himself is a member of. Respecting her feminine rights, they take the appropriate action by condemning Enlil to the underworld. He takes responsibility for what he had done but he doesn't stop loving and pursuing Ninlil, and she also remains faithful to him by doing what women have done for eternity—rescue her arrogant lover.

This process forces the couple to heal and grow. By releasing the earthly and materialistic world and turning within, their anger and injury is transformed. In the end, they return to the earth as healers and leaders who are now mature enough as god and goddess to have a healthy, loving relationship and serve their people.

Many of today's battles between the sexes, including the Me Too Movement, can lead to healing if people face what is truly happening and care to create power balances and peace between men and women. Dramas would end. Wounds would be healed, turned into growth and love.

In an effort to understand ourselves and our needs, we are constantly struggling with our ego and with many unanswered questions about who we are, where we come from, and why we are here. The feminine and intuitive, creative side of us is in conflict with the masculine, survival-based, logical side of us. Own your mistakes to break the pattern and stop the cycle.

Regardless of how hard it is to admit that you made a mistake, you must own it and move on. Do not allow it to drag you down or plant a deep thought of regret. Meditate on the lesson and realize the mistake that was made. The outer world is a reflection of our inner world. As long as we do not have peace within ourselves, there will not be peace outside of ourselves.

In your search, ask the difficult questions, be courageous and patient enough to listen to your heart's answers, to change the beliefs, thoughts and values that do not serve you or humanity. Then make a sacred contract, a promise to Spirit, listing the new beliefs, thoughts, and values you will honor from this moment forward.

For instance, during my apprenticeship with Lynn V. Andrews, at one of the school's gathering, we were presented with a Sacred Contract that contained sentences such as "I am here to honor the wisdom and magic within all life" and "I pledge to have an 'attitude of gratitude.'" Create your own sacred contract, in your own words, and sign and date it. Carve a few hours a week or a month, whatever suits your schedule, to sit at a special spot that's surrounded by inspiration. This may be a coffee shop, public park, a shopping mall, or your backyard. Review this contract, to check whether or not you're maintaining the promises you've made or if you feel the need to make some revisions. Keep your head up and walk with confidence. Spirit will guide you through it and will give you the strength to continue walking with grace and confidence.

Chapter 8

Enheduanna
Ornament of Heaven

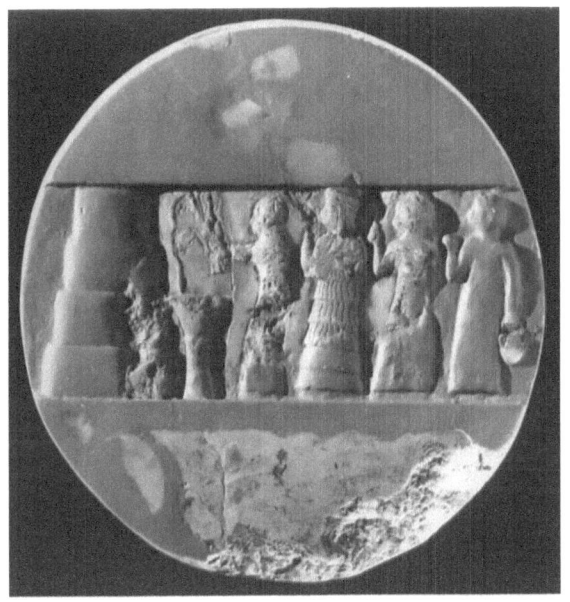

Sargon of Akkad was the son of a priestess, perhaps a sacred courtesan since he admits not knowing the identity of his father. His mother had given birth to him in secret, placed him on an island of papyrus, and locked the lid. The river carried him to a peasant who raised him. He appointed him as his gardener, and while he was a gardener, Ishtar granted Sargon her love, so he became a king who was the first to build an empire and unite northern and southern Mesopotamia. Sargon married Tashlultum, a Sumerian woman who was probably a priestess from southern Mesopotamia. She had five children with Sargon: Enheduanna, Rimush, Manishtushu, Shu-Enlil, and Ilaba'istakal.

Enheduanna was born in 2300 BC in Akkad, located in northern Mesopotamia. Wanting to expand his powers, her father decides to extend his military operations to the southern city states of Ur and Uruk. He conquers the Sumerian king, Lugalzagesi, and he designates his daughter Enheduanna as high priestess at Ur, at the temple of the moon god, Nanna. This is the most important religious office in the land and always given to someone of royal blood, such as the sister or daughter of a king. The position equals that of a king, even more so since priests and priestesses were mediators between the gods and the people.

Sargon makes this move to avoid offending the traditional Sumerians. He doesn't want them to think he plans to takeover for himself both the political and cultic titles of the southern cities. Enheduanna's job was to achieve a dynastic marriage with the gods and to extend this marriage to the people and the ruler. In this manner, the Semitic Ishtar would be syncretized and united with the Sumerian Inanna.

En means lady or lord. As the case for much of the Sumerian language, it's not gender based. It can be a woman or a man. All temples had a female priestess and male priest. If the god was male, the high priestess would be female. If the god was female, the high priest would be male. Enheduanna was the first known woman to hold the title of *En*.

Enheduanna's name translates to En (chief priest or priestess), hedu (ornament) anna (of heaven), a Sumerian title given to her at ordination. A high priestess was chosen by goat entrails. Professional oracle-priests and royal diviners would ritually sacrifice an animal and read the organs, oftentimes examining and evaluating the animal's liver, which is considered the place of the soul and number one location for all interior activity. This process, traced to Chaldea and Babylonia, matched and at times exceeded astrology as the primal means of fortune telling.

On behalf of the person who brought the animal to the temple, the royal diviners asked the gods a question, carefully constructed so that the answer wouldn't leave a false impression, and the gods engraved the answer in the entrails. This was called extispicy and the main focus of extispicy was the liver. The diviners went through an intricate and lengthy process of reading the sheep's liver, its different parts related to the heavens with the outer edge of the liver divided into the same sixteen divisions as the sky. A liver's shape, color, condition, and any evidence of disease could be used to divine the future and interpret the meaning of otherwise unclear symbols or events. The diviner then recorded these events for future reference by crafting miniature clay models of the livers they'd just analyzed.

To choose a high priestess, a ceremony was performed and the king oversaw a sacrifice of a goat. Then the diviners read the entrails and decided which of the candidates would be most agreeable to the gods for the role of high priestess. After she was chosen, the high priestess trained for a few years in seclusion to learn about her role. She was then ordained in the temple.

The day of her ordination, her hair was ceremonially combed and her clothing sanctified and placed in her father's house, where she did several sacrifices and rituals. During the evening hours, she would sit on the throne and receive gifts and jewelry such as earrings, bracelets, a turban, and a breast plate.

On the sixth day, after she ate, she left her house escorted by bridesmaids, her head covered like a bride.

In Enheduanna's case, as she entered the sacred dwelling in the giparu, a hymn she wrote was sung about this building which contained the temple of Ningal and Enheduanna's private quarters, a cemetery where the en priestesses were buried, and to the right of the cemetery, a dining area. Below it was the kitchen.

As the hours of evening arrived, Enheduanna began to settle for the night. She ate a ceremonial meal, and the elders gifted her a new dress to wear, a bed with a beautifully made spread, a chair, and a stool. While the singers sang, a close female relative washed her feet in preparation for the ritual bathing. At night, she prepared for bed, where she would perform the sacred marriage, a mystical and physical union between the divine Nanna and the human Ningal. Ningal was revered for her involvement in the sacred marriage ritual with the moon god Nanna.

The temple of Ur consisted of Nanna's temple, Ningal's temple, the storehouse, a palace, and the royal tombs. Enheduanna's office and accommodations were in the giparu, a double building for the priestess where she had special responsibility for the holy statue of Nanna's wife, Ningal. People believed that deities lived in their statues. They were therefore sacred and mighty. Only trained priests and priestesses were allowed to approach them.

As the human personification of Ningal, Enheduanna had to manage the maintenance and feeding of the goddess Ningal's statue, decorated with jewels and clothing woven and made in the temple. She presented her with meals consisting of flour, bread, and meat as well as beer, all of which was meticulously logged on clay tablets.

In her quarters was a ritual washing place for her private cultic use. In another section was a large room with a sunken waterproof floor used for ritual cleansing. Next to it was a room with a large clay brazier. The adjacent area served as the cemetery where the ens, or cult personnel and priestesses, were buried. In her poetry, Enheduanna mentions these places, saying to Inanna, "I've heaped the cools in the brazier. I've washed the sacred basin."

In the sacred marriage rite, priests and priestesses shapeshifted through a trance and visualization. They reincarnated their deity by dressing like them, thus carrying their powers and abilities. In Enheduanna's case, she became Ningal on earth. The spirit of gods would be so vivid, people could speak to it. Through this and through dream interpretations, priests and priestesses gained from the gods knowledge of the future. They also tried to help bring forth good plans and to prevent omens from happening. In her sanctuary, Enheduanna also sang and prayed for the life of the king, her father and a divine agent of the gods, and for her brothers in hopes that the gods would bestow prosperity on the land.

After the sacred marriage ceremony, the temple became Enheduanna's permanent home.

The installation of an en priestess was so significant, the year it happened was included in the royal inscription, along with the items provided for Enheduanna, such as a bed, throne, bedspreads, and so on.

Being an en priestess to the moon god was a powerful position. The moon, observed nightly for ritual purposes and for calculating time, was important for Sumerians. They followed the 29 ½-day cycle of the moon. On the day of the new moon, a festival was celebrated each month. Offerings to the moon god included bulls, sheep, lambs, goats as well as baskets of pomegranates, dates, and other fruits. The new moon in the sky resembled the crown or horns of Nanna, and so they shaped the boats, the main mode of transportation through the marshes, as the crescent shape of the new moon. During the Akitu festival of the new moon, Enheduanna traveled up the river with the Nanna statue on the crescent moon boat, called "the boat of heaven."

Young people who wanted to be a priest or priestess had to be perfect in body and come from a good family. Young boys who showed talent in the scribe schools often became priests. Girls who wanted to be priestesses also went through the literacy education given to boys, the only girls who did. The training to become a priest or priestess was arduous and difficult, but the rewards were great. In general, priests served a male god and priestesses a goddess, though some priestesses worked in the temples of male gods.

Although many classes of priestess were allowed to have sex and, in some cases, even bear children, there was one particular class that was sworn to chastity. Those priestesses not only inherited lands from their families but also lived on those properties rather than in the temple facilities like other priestesses, and if any man violated their vow of chastity, that man would be buried alive for his offense.

There were different types of priests and priestesses: sacrifice priestesses, oracle priestesses, supervising priestesses, and so on. In the temple, singers were musical priestesses charged with leading the chants and/or playing the lyre. Their role was to prepare and serve food and to entertain musically. They also performed more intimate duties which included sacred fertility rituals with male visitors to the temple to release divine fertile energy on the land, ensuring good crops and productive herds. This order of priestesses was called Nin-Gig in Sumeria. The temple also had a number of women weavers entrusted with the weaving of military and cultic apparel as well as creating items for trade.

Priestesses served as the first dentists and doctors in Mesopotamia. They treated their patients in the temple's outer court. Most priests and priestesses lived at the temple serving the gods and providing religious and medical services to the king and populace.

Priests and priestesses had many obligations and tasks, all considered honorable work that afforded them special privileges, personal stipends, and honors, luxuries, and comforts. Priests and priestesses were given equal pay.

Ordinary Mesopotamians looked to the priesthood to attain the approval of the gods, especially the patron god or goddess of their city. Each city was organized around the god's temple, which was a complex of buildings. A temple had two chief administrators. One, the en or chief priest, oversaw all sacred and religious duties of all the priests and priestesses. These priests had many tasks; some cared for the gods by feeding and clothing them, others sang, made music and wrote hymns, and others provided religious services to the people.

Different types of priests performed purifications and exorcisms, treated people medically, and prayed with them. The other chief administrator of the temple complex, the sanga, ran the business of the temple. Temples were not only places of religion but of commercial activity as well. Temples ran long distance trade networks, owned a third of the land, and provided employment to much of the city's inhabitants.

The sanga supervised all the temples' businesses. Temples

at times employed thousands of weavers to turn the wool collected from the temple's sheep into lengths of cloth. Each temple had a household staff that provided culinary and housekeeping services for the priesthood. Temples employed accountants, scribes, guards, butchers, messengers, artisans, and seamstresses. They cared for orphans and charity wards. A temple complex functioned as a small city within the city, sort of like the Vatican. It operated as the center of religious, economic, and social life. The temple served as the core of the community that crystalized into cities.

As en priestess, Enheduanna managed the extensive agricultural lands which surrounded the temple. She had to maintain the temple, monitor economic transactions as well as oversee the preparation and enactment of prescribed rituals throughout the years. To manage these duties, she had a large personal staff.

Enheduanna's influence was felt throughout the empire but her life was focused on Ur. While managing her duties, she wrote a great many hymns and poetry and was the first to break the Sumerian tradition where scribes wrote anonymously and the first person to include personal details in her writing. Although she was Akkadian, she wrote in Sumerian cuneiform, wedge-shaped writing that's formed by pressing reed-stylist on wet clay tablet. She uses clay, the only abundant natural resource in Mesopotamia, to pour out her literary heart, composing elaborate, sophisticated, beautiful, and moving literature.

Enheduanna wrote six long hymns to the goddess Inanna, a cycle of forty-two short hymns to the temples of Sumer and Akkad and two short hymns about her priestess role. This collection is generally known as "The Sumerian Temple Hymns" and they extoll the virtues of many temples. In them, she addresses the temple in the second person, treating each temple as if it were a living being with power and influence over its divine occupant. She also wrote non-devotional poems in which she reflects upon her own personal hopes and fears as well as her thoughts about the world. Each hymn ends with an identical two-line colophon, except for the hymn forty-second, the final hymn. There, instead of ending with a colophon, Enheduanna signs her name, saying she herself gave birth to this composition, something never done before. She writes,

> The person who bound this tablet together is Enheduanna
> my king something never before created
> did not this one give birth to it

Enheduanna was highly aware of the significant work she'd done. She used her spiritual power and religious background to create words which altered a whole political situation. It was part of her job to prevent a civilization from falling apart through the cultural force of poetry. She had to reconcile the Akkadian gods with the Sumerian ones. Her monumental task was to combine two deities into a single, all-powerful goddess. She accomplished this through her spiritual writings. The hymns she wrote to Inanna celebrated her individual relationship with the goddess and her strong sense of a personal relationship with the Divine Feminine.

Enheduanna continued to hold office as priestess during the reign of her brothers Rimush and Manishtushu. She also ruled through most of the reign of Manishtushu's son, Naram-Sin. This is when Sargon's ambitions are finally completed and the empire is steadfastly established. Under Naram-Sin, the empire reaches its maximum strength. He breaks with royal ideology by adopting the title "God of Akkad" and "King of the Four Quarters, King of the Universe." He is the first king depicted with a horned crown of divinity, which allows him to claim for himself the city gods' land and possessions, which was traditionally the property of the temple. Thus, he begins a trend in which the king surpasses the influence of the temple.

There were many battles during that politically turbulent time. Naram-Sin fought nine battles in one year. A ruthless ruler, Lugalanne leads the revolts against Naram-Sin in Uruk and Ur. He tries to win Enheduanna's support, to become legitimized by her by bidding against her nephew, but she rejects him, so he removes her from her position as high priestess. She's exiled from Ur to another temple and Lugalanne claims that the god Nanna had spoken that the city belonged to him and his servant. In exile, she turns to the goddess Inanna to regain her position, through prayers, song, holy words, and religious rights to alter the situation. One of the poems is called *The Exaltation of Inanna.*

"It was in your service that I first entered the holy temple,
I, Enheduanna, the highest priestess. I carried the ritual basket,
I chanted your praise.
Now I have been cast out to the place of lepers.
Day comes and the brightness is hidden around me.
Shadows cover the light, drape it in sandstorms.
My beautiful mouth knows only confusion.
Even my sex is dust.
Suen, tell An about Lugalanne and my fate!
May An undo it for me!
As soon as you tell An about it, An will release me.
The woman [Inanna] will take the destiny away from Lugalanne;

Mesopotamian Goddesses

Foreign lands and flood lie at her feet.
The woman too is exalted, and can make cities tremble.
Step forward, so that she will cool her heart for me.
I, Enheduanna, will recite a prayer to you. To you, Holy Inanna,
I shall give free vent to my tears like sweet beer!
In connection with the purification rites of holy An,
Lugalanne has altered everything of his,
and has stripped An of the E-ana.
He has not stood in awe of the greatest deity.
He has turned that temple, whose attractions were inexhaustible,
whose beauty was endless, into a destroyed temple.
While he entered before me as if he was a partner,
really he approached me out of envy.
My good divine wild cow, drive out the man, capture the man!
In the place of divine encouragement, what is my standing now?
May An extradite the land which is a malevolent rebel against your Nanna!
May An smash that city!
May Enlil curse it! May its plaintive child not be placated by his mother!
Lady, with the laments begun,
may your ship of lamentation be abandoned in hostile territory.
Must I die because of my holy songs?
My Nanna has paid no heed to me. He has not decided my case.
He has destroyed me utterly in renegade territory.
Asimbabbar has certainly not pronounced a verdict on me.
What is it to me if he has pronounced it?
What is it to me if he has not pronounced it?
He stood there in triumph and drove me out of the temple.
He made me fly like a swallow from the window;
I have exhausted my life-strength.
He made me walk through the thorn bushes of the mountains.
He stripped me of my rightful crown of the en priestess.
He gave me a knife and dagger, saying to me,
"These are appropriate ornaments for you."
Most precious lady, beloved by An, your holy heart is great;
May it be assuaged on my behalf!

Enheduanna continues with her praise and pleads, adding, "From birth you were the junior queen: how supreme you are now over Anuna, the great gods! The Anuna kiss the ground with their lips before you. But my own trial is not yet concluded, although a hostile verdict encloses me as if it were my own verdict. I did not reach out my hands to my flowered bed. I did not reveal the pronouncements of Ningal to anybody. My lady beloved of An, may your heart be calmed toward me, the brilliant priestess of Nanna! I have heaped up the coals, I the censer, and prepared the purification rites. The Esdam-kug shrine awaits you. Might your heart not be appeased toward me? Since it was full, too full for me, great exalted lady, I have recited this song for you."

Her prayers to Inanna are answered with victories in battle that put down the rebellion. This allows her royal nephew Naram-Sin to successfully unite Sumer and Akkad for several years. As a result, Enheduanna is restored to her post as priestess of Nanna, thanks, she says, to her "Queen" Inanna. Her reign lasts for over forty years.

It's not known how Enheduanna died. She was buried in the temple complex of giparu along with her personnel. After her death, a hymn was devoted to her by an anonymous composer, indicating that she may have been venerated as a deity herself. Her hymns were copied by scribes for at least five centuries and her writings are believed to have influenced the merger of the Sumerian Inanna with Akkadian Ishtar.

In 1927, the British archaeologist Sir Leonard Woolley found the now-famous Enheduanna calcite disk, which she commissioned, in his excavations at the Sumerian site of Ur. The three inscriptions on the disc identify the four figures depicted: Enheduanna, her estate manager Adda, her hair dresser Ilum Palilis, and her scribe Sagadu. She's wearing a ruffled dress and a brimmed turban, a sign of her office. The royal inscription on the disc reads: "Enheduanna, zirru-priestess, wife of the god Nanna, daughter of Sargon, king of the world, in the temple of the goddess Innana." The figure of Enheduanna is placed prominently on the disc, emphasizing her importance in relation to the others and, further, her position of great power and influence on the culture of her time. The disk is currently on display at the Penn Museum in Philadelphia.

Woolley also uncovered the temple complex where the priestesses were buried in a special cemetery. Scholar Paul Kriwaczek writes, "Records suggest that offerings continued to be made to these dead priestesses. That one of the most striking artifacts, physical proof of Enheduanna's existence, was found in a layer dateable to many centuries after her lifetime, makes it likely that she in particular was remembered and honored long after the fall of the dynasty that had appointed her to the management of the temple."

During Enheduanna's time, there was still a permanent and necessary place for women in different cults in contrast with the major religions of today which has not allowed priestesses in position for the last two-thousand years. In these early years in Sumer, it was completely normal to have women in the highest religious positions of the society.

Enheduanna had a considerable political and religious role in Ur. She sets the earliest surviving verbal account of an individual's consciousness of her inner life, offering a first-person perspective on the last times women in Western society held religious and civil power. She is best known for her works:

Inninsagurra (The Great-Hearted Mistress), *Ninmesarra* (The Exaltation of Inanna), and *Inninmehusa* (the Goddess of the Fearsome Powers). All three are hymns to the goddess Inanna. These hymns helped the people of Akkad redefine the gods and provided fundamental religious equality.

She wrote during the rise of the agricultural civilization, when gathering territory and wealth, warfare, and patriarchy were making their marks. It has been written that, as secular males acquired more power, religious beliefs had evolved from what was probably a central female deity in Neolithic times to a central male deity by the Bronze Age. Female power and freedom sharply diminished during the Assyrian era, the period in which the first evidence of laws requiring the public veiling of elite women was made.

During a radio broadcast by Catholic Answers, a caller told a story to Tim Staples, director of Apologetics. He said that several years ago he asked a Jewish scholar, "Why did God choose men to be rabbis?" The Jewish scholar's response was that God knew that women are more spiritually advanced than men, that the most dangerous animal on earth is an immoral male and therefore men are more in need of association in leadership in the church and spiritual organizations. The caller then asked Tim Staples, "Is that the same reason he chose men as priests and apostles?"

Mr. Staples said that while that was an interesting angle, it's not the angle that Jesus or the Church takes. He referenced a doctrine written in 1976 that states six reasons why women can't be ordained, the first being that Jesus Christ was a man, a priest, prophet and king. He said, "It is the man who fittingly delivers the seed, the word of God, and as a priest, he is the mediator between God and men. He acts in the place of God and God is the one who ultimately delivers the seed which is the word of God. He is the transcendent authority in the image of the Father."

The priest acts as persona Christi, who becomes Christ and God for people. That's why the priests says "I absolve you of your sins" in the confessional. He says "This is my body" when he gives the Eucharis. But God didn't give this type of power and privilege to priesthood, to men over women. Men did. They wrote everything and instituted a patriarchal system which empowers men and keeps women beneath them. Before the patriarchal system, women could be ordained and many were.

According to Max Shadu, "Barring women from ritual leadership and religious authority has been a key focus in the drive to undermine female power. Scriptures of the 'major' religions often ban priestesses and female religious authority, either explicitly or through stories demonizing their power. Over centuries, male authorities carefully selected and edited the religious canon so as to erase traditions of female leadership (such as the Gnostic scriptures naming Mary Magdalene as the foremost Christian disciple)."

Enheduanna is the model of not giving up. She shows how a personal relationship with God/dess can sustain you. She teaches about keeping your faith. Through prayer, her devotional chants, she was able to achieve the outcome she wanted. Her compositions, though only rediscovered in modern times, remained models of petitionary prayer for centuries. Through the Babylonians, they influenced and inspired the prayers and psalms of the Hebrew Bible and the Homeric hymns of Greece.

Through them, faint echoes of Enheduanna, the first named literary author in history, can even be heard in the hymnody of the early Christian church.

The ordination of women to ministerial or priestly office is an increasingly common practice among some major religious groups of the present times, as it was of several pagan religions of antiquity and, some scholars argue, in early Christian practice. While Jesus did not ordain anyone, he did call both women and men to discipleship. There is significant evidence that there were churches in the fourth to sixth centuries that remained in communion with Rome and also had women priests.

Dr. Giorgio Otranto, Director of the Institute for Classical and Christian Studies at the University of Bari, Italy, discovered iconographic evidence of women presiding over the Eucharist in ancient catacomb frescos. St. Paul says that all Christians, both male and female, share in and make up Christ's risen body, not by imaging the maleness of Jesus, but by participating in the paschal mystery through Baptism.

Galatians 3:28, an early Christian Baptismal formula, tells us "There is no longer Jew nor Greek, slave nor free, male and female…all are one in Christ Jesus." Both women and men are the image of Christ. Nearly all Protestant denominations, as well as reformed Judaism, have women serving as priests, ministers, or rabbis.

The spiritual power and the wisdom of women are greatly needed in our world today. For our world to benefit from a woman's gifts, we need to openly recognize them as healers, spiritual teachers, and leaders. And women need to choose to harness their power and get to work helping to protect our world for their welfare, their children and grandchildren, and for the next several generations.

Many women are already harnessing their power in churches and elsewhere. A new report shows that the share of women in the ranks of American clergy has doubled, and sometimes tripled, in some denominations over the last two decades. But women continue to lag behind clergymen in leading their churches.

Susan Frederick-Gray, president of the Unitarian Universalist Association, credits the increase of clergywomen to a decision by her denomination's General Assembly in 1970 to call for women to serve in ministry and policymaking roles. As of this year, 60 percent of UUA clergy are women. She says that women's leadership is necessary at a time of decline for many religions, adding, "The decline is not the responsibility of women, but maybe we will be the hope for the future."

But how does one start with this path, if she hasn't done so already? One way is through rituals, which are mindful, purposeful actions you choose to make habitual because they improve your life. Ritual plays a major part in primitive cultures, although people from those cultures did not consider their rituals different from so-called practical activity. It is rather an attempt to influence or harmonize oneself with the course of nature by dramatized or symbolic enactment of such fundamental events as the daily rising and setting of the sun. Ritual is the great mythical themes that, in these cultures, take the place of religious doctrines. Ritual, as found in primitive religions, might therefore be described as an art form where people can express and celebrate humanity's meaningful participation in the affairs of the universe and of God.

In cultures in which this type of feeling about the world prevails, no department of life is specifically recognizable as religion. Everything is permeated by religion; indeed, religion is so involved with everyday life that it is impossible to distinguish the sacred from the secular. Only greater and lesser degrees of the sacred exist. Religion as a specific activity does not exist, and members of such cultures would have the greatest difficulty in talking about their religion.

Not including prayer and meditation, what are the rituals in your daily life? For me, it's taking a one-hour walk outdoors, reading a passage from Lynn V. Andrews' *Walk in Balance*, doing yoga, cooking, and even cleaning, a time which allows me to do deep breathing and to reflect on projects I'm working on.

Describe your daily rituals in your journal, looking for the symbolism in your ritual. Spirit is a feeling rather than an idea; the language most appropriate to it consists of concepts noticeable through symbolism. Symbols such as family photos, a cross, a Buddhist statue, or a poem helps connect you to what matters to you. Create a sacred space in your home and work with symbols that are significant to you. This will invoke mana, a pervasive supernatural or magical power, into the rituals you choose to create and maintain in your life.

Chapter 9

Ninkasi
Goddess of Beer

Ninkasi is the daughter of Enki, god of wisdom, and Ninhursag, lady of the mountains. She's one of eight gods and goddesses her mother gave birth to in order to heal her father after he'd eaten the eight plants and fallen ill. Each of Ninhursag's eight offspring had supernatural powers to benefit humanity. When Enki said, "My mouth hurts," Ninhursag gave birth to Ninkasi out of it, the goddess of beer, made to satisfy desires and lighten hearts. Ninkasi's name translates to "the lady who fills the mouth."

Beer was a staple in Mesopotamians' diet and a favorite drink from prehistoric times. Started and cultivated by women, brewing beer began in the small village of Godi Tepe, which later became an important town and fortress along the famous Silk Road trade route. Ebla, another Sumerian outpost, brewed great quantities of beer using different recipes. These earliest beers were possibly concocted with the aid of barley that was extracted from bread. The fermentation method apparent in grains, which may have been left out unattended, could have motivated the creation of both wine and beer.

Because Mesopotamians boiled fresh water to make beer, killing bacteria and waterborne disease, it was a healthier drink than water from canals, which could be contaminated by animal waste. And it had nutrients other beverages did not. The varieties of beer were endless, brewed to different strengths and with different flavors. Although beer was cautiously filtered, it was drunk through a straw, which Sumerians invented specifically to keep from consuming residue in the beer.

Women initially brewed beer in the home until commercial production of the beverage began and men started taking over. Ninkasi symbolizes the role women played in brewing and preparing beverages in ancient Mesopotamia. But this was not a light matter. Beer consumption was an important marker for societal and civilized virtues, created to make the heart feel light. Beer was considered to have healing and uplifting elements which could advance one's life.

In the *Epic of Gilgamesh*, the wild man Enkidu "did not know how to eat bread nor had he ever learned to drink beer!" with the latter phrase suggesting that drinking beer was seen as a "quality" of a civilized person. Also Siduri, a tavern keeper, attempts to dissuade Gilgamesh in his quest for immortality, urging him to be content with the simple pleasures of life. She has a long and wise conversation with him where she explains the difficulties of the journey but directs him to the ferryman nonetheless.

Beer was offered to the gods and goddesses and to the dead during drink rituals. In the poem *Inanna and the God of Wisdom*, the goddess Inanna and the god of wisdom Enki get drunk together before Inanna requests of him to give her the powerful essentials she needs for her city. In the poem *Enki and Ninmah*, the goddess Ninhursag loses respect when Enki defeats her in a drinking game. The drinker showed signs of weakness when he or she weren't able to hold their drink. But in Mesopotamia, people from all ranks drank beer. Employers provided workers with daily rations of it.

Ninkasi and beer is associated with healing. She, a lover of beer, made fresh beer every day, using the best ingredients. Her priestesses sang a hymn to her as they worked. The hymn doubles as a praise song and instructions for how to brew beer. Few people were literate during that time, and the *Hymn to Ninkasi* allowed an easy way to remember the recipe which was passed down by master brewers to their apprentices.

Ninkasi's clergy began the recipe with flowing water, then by making Bappir—twice-baked barley bread—and mixing it with honey and dates. Once the bread cools on reed mats, it's mixed with water and wine before it's put on the fermenter. After the brew finishes the fermentation process, it's placed in the filtering vat "which makes a pleasant sound" and then placed "appropriately on a collector vat" from which the filtered beer is then poured into jars. According to the hymn, the pouring of the beer is "like the onrush of the Tigris and Euphrates." Like those two rivers, beer brought life to those who drank it.

Hymn to Ninkasi

Borne of the flowing water,
Tenderly cared for by the Ninhursag,
Borne of the flowing water,
Tenderly cared for by the Ninhursag,
Having founded your town by the sacred lake,
She finished its great walls for you,
Ninkasi, having founded your town by the sacred lake,
She finished its walls for you,
Your father is Enki, Lord Nidimmud,
Your mother is Ninti, the queen of the sacred lake.
Ninkasi, your father is Enki, Lord Nidimmud,
Your mother is Ninti, the queen of the sacred lake.
You are the one who handles the dough [and] with a big shovel,
Mixing in a pit, the beerbread with sweet aromatics,
Ninkasi, you are the one who handles the dough [and] with a big shovel,
Mixing in a pit, the beerbread with wine and honey,
You are the one who bakes the beerbread in the big oven,
Puts in order the piles of hulled grains,

Mesopotamian Goddesses

Ninkasi, you are the one who bakes the beerbread in the big oven,
Puts in order the piles of hulled grains,
You are the one who waters the malt set on the ground,
The noble dogs keep away even the potentates,
Ninkasi, you are the one who waters the malt set on the ground,
The noble dogs keep away even the potentates,
You are the one who soaks the malt in a jar,
The waves rise, the waves fall.
Ninkasi, you are the one who soaks the malt in a jar,
The waves rise, the waves fall.
You are the one who spreads the cooked mash on large reed mats,
Coolness overcomes,
Ninkasi, you are the one who spreads the cooked mash on large reed mats,
Coolness overcomes,
You are the one who holds with both hands the great sweetwort,
Brewing [it] with honey [and] wine
(You the sweetwort to the vessel)
Ninkasi, (...)(You the sweetwort to the vessel)
The filtering vat, which makes a pleasant sound,
You place appropriately on a large collector vat.
Ninkasi, the filtering vat, which makes a pleasant sound,
You place appropriately on a large collector vat.
When you pour out the filtered beer of the collector vat,
It is [like] the onrush of Tigris and Euphrates.
Ninkasi, you are the one who pours out the filtered beer of the collector vat,
It is [like] the onrush of Tigris and Euphrates.

April Holloway stated that alcohol was not consumed in the same way as it is today. In fact, in ancient times, alcohol was seen as an important medicinal ingredient and as an essential part of the diet. From the moment the first alcoholic beverages were discovered, man has used it as a medicine. Apart from the stress relieving, relaxing nature that alcohol has on the body and mind, alcohol is an antiseptic and in higher doses has anesthetizing effects. But it is a combination of alcohol and natural botanicals which creates a far more effective medicine and has been used as such for thousands of years. It is the origin of the most famous toast, "Let's drink to health," which exists in many languages around the world.

Used in moderation, beer has many health benefits. A Finnish study found that each bottle of beer you drink reduces the risk of developing kidney stones by 40 percent. Beer is good for digestion, containing a soluble fiber which isn't present in wine. This fiber also lowers the levels of cholesterol. Beer increases one's vitamin B levels, can contribute to higher bone density, and can cure insomnia. According to studies, beer reduces the risk of a heart attack, prevents blood clots, and boosts memory. It helps combat stress, and it's a great cold remedy. It also makes skin more beautiful. Some believe that, based on a scientific review, swapping beverages for beer may actually be a sensible way to diet.

Throughout history, all around the world, people made recipes that heal and are used in various religious rituals to reach higher consciousness. The majority of these substances are considered illegal in most countries, used as the scapegoat for all the failures that occur in society, while other substances that truly diminish the mind are legal. Everything is about balance and harmony and as long as we have a relationship with and understanding of the law of nature, we don't need to be told to take certain patented pills when the Earth has provided us with all the nutrients we need.

What happened over these thousands of years? How did people disconnect from using food and drink in moderation? Doctors and nutritionists constantly tell people what to eat and when. Rather than listen to what their own bodies are telling them, people tend to listen to these messages, which by the way, change regularly. One day eating breakfast is the best thing for your body. Another day skipping breakfast could help you lose weight. Some tell you how harmful coffee is; others hand you a list of its health benefits.

Young girls are particularly susceptible to developing body image issues because of the tall, slim, and light-skinned figures they're bombarded with on a daily basis. The proliferation of sexualized images of girls and young women in advertising, merchandising, and media is harmful to girls' self-image and healthy development. On the other extreme, the glamorization of obesity is also harmful.

Do you listen to your body when it tells you it's not hungry in the morning, or do you force it to eat breakfast just because you've been told myths about why it's better to do so? Did you know that orange juice's fabled health benefits were promoted by nutritionists, fruit producers, marketers, and the government who credited orange juice with curing everything from scurvy to listlessness and even a rare blood condition called acidosis?

There has been much mental conditioning complicating simple matters of health and wellness. People can benefit from taking an active part in creating their own health. Too many are passive, expecting someone else to do it for them. Going back to our own natural way of living would make us all healthier.

One author's advice for good health is to stop consuming two substances introduced into our diets in the 1850s—sugar and polyunsaturated vegetables—and avoid the cures introduced after World War II. The inconvenient truth is that this means eliminating almost all processed foods from your diet.

Wallace D. Wattles recommended to "never eat until you have earned hunger." He said that it will not hurt you in the least to go hungry for a short time, but it will surely hurt you to eat when you are not hungry. When you earn your hunger, you will not demand unnatural or unhealthy foods.

Your body is your sanctuary. Food is the fuel for this incredible machine. Be a conscious eater with every meal, not an obsessed devotee of food. Abandon counting calories, stepping on scales, going on diets, and being at a perfect weight. Instead, trust yourself to have self-control and not over-indulge as you relish what's on your plate. And keep your body moving.

Chapter 10

Gula
The Great Healer

After the Great Flood, Gula helped breathe life into mankind. She saw the terrible destruction wrought by the Flood and, since she'd lost her husband to the Netherworld, she became interested in caring for the sick and wounded in the Great Above. She became patroness of herbs, healing, and life.

Initially Gula was a Sumerian deity known as Bau, or Baba, goddess of dogs. Gula's cylinder seals portray her always with a dog, sometimes seated, and surrounded by stars. Dog figurines dedicated to the goddess were found in the Kassite temple at Isin and in temples at other Babylonian sites. People noticed that when dogs licked their sores, they seemed to heal faster, and so dogs became associated with healing and Bau transformed into a healing deity. When her worship spread from the city of Lagash to Isin, she became known as Ninisina, "Lady of Isin." As her worship spread across Sumer and the entire region of Mesopotamia, she became known during the Ur II Period (2047-1750 BCE) and up until today as Gula, the great healer.

The daughter of the great god Anu and Antu, Gula's consorts range from Ninurta, the healer god, to Pabilsag, divine judge, to the god of agriculture, Abu. Her children included two sons, Damu and Ninazu, and a daughter, Gunurra, all healing deities.

Damu, the chief Sumerian god of healing, combined the mystical and scientific tactics of healing to cure illness. Associated with transformation and transition, he's often mentioned with his mother Gula, the supreme healer, in chants for healing. Damu was thought to be the intercessor through which her power reached physicians. Her other son Ninazu, who carried a rod entwined with serpents, was linked with serpents, the underworld, and healing. This symbol was adopted by the

Egyptians, later the Greeks, and today, one sees the caduceus in doctor's offices and medical practices around the world as the sign of Hippocrates, the father of medicine.

A cult center for Gula, the city of Isin is thought to have served as a training center for physicians, who were then assigned to temples in different cities as needed. Doctors usually made house calls but also treated patients at the temples. Women and men could both be doctors, with more female physicians in Sumer than elsewhere.

Mesopotamian doctors had offices, beds for patients, and pharmacological equipment. There were two types of doctors: asu practiced therapeutic and scientific medicine, consisting of surgical and herbal treatments. Asipu practiced magic and religious medicine. The text of the Code of Hammurabi (c. 1700 BCE) differentiates religious healers in two classes: diviners, baru, who practiced hepatoscopy and made prognoses and exorcists, and ashipu, who determined what offense to the gods or demons had brought about the disease. People viewed illness and disease as punishments from the gods or an omen, a way to get a person back on the right track. They also attributed illness and disease to evil spirits, demons, or angry dead spirits.

Both types of healers gave physical examinations to look for telling symptoms and omens and were trained in schools connected with temples of the goddess of medicine and healing, Gula. They were educated using a combination of clay tablet textbooks, the equivalent of rounds, and practical experience; asu focused more on the patients' accounts of their illnesses than on physical examination, which was what the ashipu focused on. The two types of healers worked in peaceful coexistence rather than competing and Mesopotamians regarded the two with equal respect.

These doctors practiced dentistry and at times presided at births. While the midwives delivered babies, records show that a doctor was paid a fee for his or her service (more for the birth of a male child than a female), which may have been to ease labor pains or ward off evil spirits such as the demon Lamashtu who killed or carried off infants.

Medical books from the library of Ashurbanipal indicate that doctors had a remarkable amount of medical knowledge and applied this repeatedly in caring for their patients and appeasing the gods and the spirits of the dead. People accredited this knowledge to Gula as a gift from the gods so they regularly called upon her for help with conception through writings that summoned fertility, particularly when they felt that a supernatural spirit was interfering. She oftentimes was able to restore the person to health.

Gula is summoned for curses as well as for healing. Her fury could bring earthquakes and storms. An engraving on Nebuchadnezzar I's memorial reads in part how, if anyone should ruin or remove it, "May Ninurta, the king of heaven and earth, and Gula, the bride of E-Sharra, destroy his landmark and blot out his seed." Gula's name is engraved elsewhere in the same fashion. Thus, she was nicknamed "Queen of the Tempest" and "She Who Makes Heaven Tremble."

Many ceramic statuettes of her sacred animal, the dog, were dedicated to her at her sanctuaries by people who had been blessed by her. Dogs wandered freely within the sanctuary and played a key role in the healing rituals, although specific details of what they did are uncertain. Perhaps they played a part in ritual sacrifice since there were over thirty dogs buried beneath the ramp leading to Gula's temple at Isin. Or these dogs could have simply been temple dogs, esteemed with burial at

Mesopotamian Goddesses

the entrance. Ceramic dog figures buried at numerous sites, at doorways, and at thresholds were frequently inscribed with Gula's name to protect homes from evil and harm.

The status of female deities began to diminish during the reign of Hammurabi (1792-1750 BCE) and afterward, when male gods dominated the religious arena. That wasn't the case with Gula, however, whose worship remained with the same respect. Adoration of Gula continued well into the Christian period, and in the Near East, Gula was as prevalent as many well-known divinities. Her cult declined little by little until, by the end of the first millennium CE, she had been forgotten.

Our body is not only our sanctuary but our greatest friend. Prior to getting a physical ailment, there's usually a message that we miss because we don't listen to our intuition. Whatever is going on in our life, our body mirrors it. Rather than review our life to understand where our dis ease is coming from, we quickly head to the doctor to remove the ailment through medication or removing that body part. People will even keep returning to the doctor when the doctor can't help them. I've heard so many stories of people having stomach pains or other ailments where the doctors prescribed a dozen tests but couldn't find the problem. In such cases, the only person who knows the cause and the cure is the patient.

Therapy is within us and everyone has the potential to heal, but we've forgotten these things. We forgot the value of working with pen and paper, stones and crystals, with drums and flutes, something that the ancient Sumerians used thousands of years ago to relieve anxiety and stress, raise our vibrations and create spiritual grounding. We forgot how to journey, which, similar to shamanism, the ancient Sumerians did to reach the heavens and the netherworld in order to purify the soul and experience transformation and a rebirth, as described in *Inanna's Descent to the Underworld*.

We kept losing our ancient ways until the late twentieth century, when critics stated that Western medicine had become victim to a movement focused solely on professionalism. These critics claimed that numerous medical schools and residency programs teach physicians to deal with medical problems solely in response to their symptoms without taking into account the precise psychological and personal history of the patient. Physicians tended to overlook the human side of disease. To re-humanize medicine, narrative medicine was created, with Columbia University Medical Center beginning the first program in Narrative Medicine.

An increasing number of people are turning to alternative forms of medicine to reduce stress, relieve chronic pain, and treat other ailments. Traditional, indigenous, and folkloric practices, such as shamanism, which has many similarities to ancient Mesopotamian healing practices, use natural resources and products that have worked for millennia. In ancient Mesopotamia, many saw states of illness as illnesses sent by the gods in retaliation for human sin and misbehavior, and generally, diseases had to be alleviated or removed by reconciling with the gods or by expelling the disease through the use of witchcraft from the body of the patient. This typically involved either religious prayers or incantations.

Similarly, shamans believe that healing on the spiritual level can prevent conditions from appearing in the body or cure the condition. Shamans see a disease such as cancer as an intrusion into an energy body. It has its own spirit—not good or bad energy but an energy seeking to make a home inside the human which it feeds off of. A shaman skilled in this area will work with the spirit of the cancer, either by negotiating with it to go away or fighting it in some way.

The way to heal is to understand that Spirit sometimes uses illness for us to evolve. What is the lesson? What is the earth telling us? What does it want us to remember? Perhaps it wants us to realize we need to rest, to have more joy, to breathe more deeply, exhale more lovingly. Perhaps it wants us to recall the sacredness of a walk, a physical activity that is not part of many peoples' regular ritual; the sacredness of gardening, preparing a meal and doing yoga naturally when cleaning the house. In Iraq, women didn't use a mop to wipe the floors. They used a rag and bent their bodies over in a popular yoga posture called downward facing dog. It is a great exercise and one needn't go to a yoga studio to do it.

Or perhaps the illness wants us to remember that death is closer than we think and not to take life for granted and squander it on meaningless experiences. As soon as the lesson is understood and resolved, the illness has the chance to balance itself and transform into a healthy situation, even if that balance and transformation means the illness itself is not entirely cured.

It's important to respect and study modern medical advances as we embrace and connect with nature and realize that our spiritual life plays an important role in having a balanced and healthy mind, heart, and body. But it's equally important that we don't give our power away to physicians by simply accepting the medications they prescribe and the procedures and surgeries they recommend. Being in continuous alignment with our own meaning and purpose in life helps us weed out and keep out individuals, circumstances, and contracts that do not honor our highest self. Beliefs that we inherited from society, our ancestors, and people in our close familiar environment as children sometimes contribute to our dis ease, so once we become aware of what is contributing to our dis ease, we must take the proper steps to dust them off and move into a lifestyle where healthy foods and natural cures are readily available and exercise, relaxation, and rejuvenation are a regular part of life.

Chapter 11

Nanshe
Goddess of Social Justice

Nanshe is one of eight healing gods born of Enki, god of wisdom and fresh water, and Ninhursag, the Mother Goddess, after Enki eats from the forbidden plants and becomes ill. She was made to heal her father's neck, then assigned dominion over the Persian Gulf, on which floated her father's inspirational sea shrine. She also ensures that shipments of fish reach the mainland, and she has a close relationship with animals. In one hymn, she converses with ravens and pelicans, among other species.

Nanshe's consort was Haia, god of storerooms, and her vizier was Hendursag, who was in charge of judging people's deeds and transgressions. Nanshe performed multiple functions such as granting fertility, fishing, and overseeing social justice and prophecies. During the time of Gudea (2144—2124 BC), hymns to Nanshe show that she was a broadly worshiped goddess of social justice. Nanshe nurtured orphans, provided for widows, gave advice to those in debt, and took in refugees from war-torn areas. She settled disputes and handled court cases amongst mortals. Several gods assisted her with maintaining a positive social balance and Nisaba, sometimes portrayed as her sister, was her chief scribe.

On the first day of the New Year, a great festival was held at her temple. People came from all over the land to seek her wisdom and aid, to settle some legal dispute, gain a vision of the future, and interpret dreams. Visitors cleansed themselves in the river of ordeals and then, if worthy, were allowed to be part of the audience with the goddess.

Nanshe sat on the holy thrones with the other prominent gods and was seen as a goddess of protection, as she expressed special concern for vulnerable members of society. As the goddess of prophecy, she determined the future by oneiromancy, the process of interpreting dreams. Her priests were granted the gift of prophecy after performing certain rituals that involved the end of life and resurrection. Despite the ritual, she's not depicted as a life-death-rebirth deity in any known hymns or myths. The most famous receiver of Nanshe's generosity was Gudea, the governor of Lagash, a pious Mesopotamian ruler who built temples and worked hard to preserve the literary and religious traditions of Sumer. The Mesopotamian statue of the

Mesopotamian Goddesses

robed man, hands clasped in prayer, is Gudea. He was worshiped during the later Ur III Period (2047-1700 BCE) as a god.

One day, Gudea has a dream where he sees a man with tremendous stature. He has a divine crown on his head, the wings of a lion-headed bird, and a hurricane as the lower part of his body. Lions are sitting to his right and left. The man demands that Gudea build his temple, but Gudea doesn't completely understand the meaning. In the morning, a woman shows up holding a gold stylus and reviewing a clay tablet that portrays the starry heaven. A hero comes along with a tablet of lapis lazuli and he draws on it a plan of a house. He also puts bricks in a brick mold in front of Gudea together with a carrying basket. Meanwhile, a donkey waits impatiently as he paws the ground.

The dream continues in the morning, where Gudea rides a boat to visit Nanshe so she can interpret this dream. During the journey, he stops at several important shrines along the way to offer sacrifices and prayers to their deities to get their support. The boat arrives at the quay of Nina, where Nanshe lives, and Gudea walks into the court of the temple and tells Nanshe his dream.

Nanshe interprets the dream for him, telling him that the man with great stature is her brother Ningirsu, commanding him to build the temple. The morning is Ningishzida, Gudea's personal god, rising like the sun. The woman studying a clay tablet is Nisaba, the goddess of writing, who instructs Gudea to build the house in harmony with the holy stars. The hero holding the tablet is the architect god Nindub drawing the temple plan. The carrying basket and brick mold are the bricks from the Eninnu temple. The male donkey is Gudea himself, who is impatient to carry out his task.

Gudea wakes up from the dream, prays, gives thanks to

Nanshe, and shares his dream with his people. He asks for their support and they respond with a spirit of eagerness. The Gudea cylinders show Nanshe as the wise and helpful goddess for Mesopotamians. When compared to her sister Inanna, people favor her since she is notably silent. She's never described as trivial, egotistical, or selfish.

A hymn to Nanshe

> 20-31 She is concerned for the orphan and concerned for the widow. She does not forget the man who helps (?) others, she is a mother for the orphan; Nance, a carer for the widow, who always finds advice for the debt-slave; the lady who gives protection for refugees. She seeks out a place for the weak. She swells his collecting basket for him; she makes his collecting vessel profitable for him. For the righteous maiden who has taken her path, Nance chooses a young man of means. Nance raises a secure house like a roof over the widow who could not remarry.

In the hymn, she is known as the Lady of the Storeroom and, in this capacity, made sure that weights and measures are correct.

> 223-231: The guarantor of boundaries, the expert in (?) righteous words, lady, wise woman who founded Lagac ... with Jatumdug. ... righteous words for (?) Nance. The exalted lady whose commands are ... the lady who like Enlil determines fates, who is seated on the throne of Sirara — she, the pure one, looks at her powers.

251-255 My lady, your divine powers are mighty powers, surpassing all other divine powers; Nance, there are no divine powers matching your powers. An, the king, looks joyfully at you, as you sit with Enlil on the throne-dais where the fates are to be determined. Father Enki determined a fate for you. Nance, child born in Eridug, sweet is your praise.

Nanshe has two major symbols, both of which are also seen in Christian folklore. The fish represents her original role as a water and fishing goddess. The pelican, said in folklore to rip open its own chest to feed its young, represents her role as a protector and caregiver.

Nanshe was in service to something larger than herself. In our youth, we believe that the world is much more beautiful than most adults see it. As we get older, it becomes a lot harder to believe in our stories, in ourselves, in our healing powers. For women, part of the reason is that she's the one who gives birth and raises her children. Later in life, she may become the caregiver for a parent. Her hopes and dreams slip away, turning into dust.

But what if women who love to work had the support of women who love to stay at home and vice versa, not just through superficial words and socializing but through actions. In my shamanic training, we learned that there were two types of mother energies, Rainbow Mother and Nurturing Mother. My teacher, Lynn V. Andrews, described them as follows:

Rainbow Mother is the energy of the poet, the dancer, the weaver, and the seer. She is completely misunderstood in our society, a world that does not support its artists, its writers and thinkers. She wants to dream and inspire people to health and well-being and routine wilts her. Rainbow Mother is usually seen as a misfit, a person on the fringes. They often live in chaos because they are always in the dream state. They become frustrated, unfulfilled, perhaps even alcoholic or drug addicts because of the expectations of others, because they are afraid of living life fully as their beautiful Rainbow selves…

Nurturing Mother is someone who loves routine, gets married, raises her children and is a pillar of society. She is the grandmother of the gods. Yet she likes to know what you're doing all of the time and sets great expectations on the world around you. When a Nurturing Mother reaches midlife and finds that her children are grown and there is no one left to nurture, then her opposite energy, Death Mother, comes close and tries to take her away.

If you choose not to look at Rainbow Mother's and Nurturing Mother's opposites—Crazy Woman and Death Mother—and honor their power, they can easily overpower you. Then, Lynn says, you will be consumed by madness, depression, or even death. I go into more details about these mother energies in my four-part memoir series, *Healing Wisdom for a Wounded World: My Life-Changing Journey Through a Shamanic School*.

What mother energy are you? What mother energy is your mother, father, husband, partner, son, and daughter? Take time to think about that and write down your answers. Or perhaps have a conversation with those individuals to get a clearer understanding of who they really are. Understanding the mother energies of our loved ones can make a major impact on our relationships.

When women understand the different mother energies, a Nurturing Mother will recognize that a Rainbow Mother is going crazy because she doesn't have any free time. Perhaps she could step in and offer to nurture Rainbow Mother's children for certain time periods. An act like this could create the strongest bonds and help heal families and communities because it's true that it takes a village to raise a child. On the other hand, when a Rainbow Mother recognizes that a Nurturing Mother is feeling depressed and lonely, she can find creative ways to make her feel wanted, needed, and appreciated. Maybe she could seek the Nurturing Mother's advice on a matter or include her in her circle of friends.

Many women feel that this kind of sisterhood is missing in their lives. In our culture, women have fallen into the vicious cycle of criticizing and shaming each other. They've allowed their stories to involve disloyalty, pettiness, and jealousy, rather than standing up for and protecting each other. In the past, they were the spiritual leaders and would make policies in the tribe. They built homes together. In the 1940s in Baghdad, my father and mother in their early years of marriage lived in one house with four other families. My mother became close friends with the women and said of that experience, "Four families used to live in peace in one house. Nowadays, two people can't live together under one roof."

Women have forgotten their power, their walk and purpose on this earth, but they are bringing that power back. We're realizing that our power is in our togetherness, especially in circle work. Building circles benefits us, our families, and our communities. We can then work constructively and creatively rather than tear each other apart to advance ourselves. By creating a different story, we decode the mental infrastructure of our mythology and we offer an alternative. Old, disempowering stories deteriorate into new empowering ones about self, the world, and the people around us. Then our acts become not only spiritual but political, transforming the world that we live in so that the new generation can experience a different story.

Chapter 12

Semiramis
Gift of the Sea

Semiramis has one historical story and several legendary ones. We'll start with the historical story, which is based on four principal artifacts found by archaeologists that mention her name. Born Sammuramat, meaning gift of the sea, this beautiful and powerful woman might have been Babylonian. She became a queen when she married King Shamshi-Adad V, the ruler of the Assyrian Empire (823 to 811 BC.) who was named after the god Adad, the storm and rain god in the northwest Semitic and ancient Mesopotamian religions. He was the grandson of Assyria's great ruler, Ashurnasirpal II, a flamboyant monarch who built a magnificent palace in Nimrud in the early ninth century BC. This event is commemorated by the Banquet Stele, which recorded thousands of guests and a celebration that lasted for ten days. Ashurnasirpal II stabilized the empire, putting down revolts with a level of cruelty that he made no attempt to hide.

The empire that Ashurnasirpal II's grandson inherited may have been stable and wealthy, but it did not stay that way for long. King Shamshi-Adad V appears to have spent a great deal of resources defeating his rebellious elder brother, who wanted to take the throne and thus created a civil war. The first years of Shamshi-Adad's reign are definitely a struggle. He ends up campaigning against southern Mesopotamia and stipulates a treaty with the Babylonian King Marduk-zakir-shumi I. In 814 BC, he wins a battle against the Babylonian king but much of the resources at his disposal have dissipated. The Assyrian Empire is weak and unstable financially and politically.

His wife Sammuramat, who bores him a son, Adad-nirari III, accompanies her husband, the king, on at least one military campaign. When the king dies, the son is too young to rule, so it's up to Queen Sammuramat to restore stability to Assyria through her regency. During her five-year reign (81–806 BCE), she provides the nation with strength and stability by securing the kingdom during an era when women rulers were not permitted to have such power or authority. She controls the vast New Assyrian

Empire, which stretched from the Caucasus Mountains in the north to the Arabian Peninsula in the south, and western Iran in the east to Cyprus in the west. She defeats the Medes and annexes their territory, conquers the Armenians and, according to some historians, built the banks at Babylon on the Euphrates River.

By the time Adad-nirari III came of age (he would reign until 783 BC), Sammuramat had exercised a degree of political power and impressed her subjects with her strength and steadiness, as the stele at Assur shows. During her son's reign, she also accompanied him for some military campaigns. A pillar in the city of Ashur has this inscription on it: *Stele of Sammuramat, queen of Shamsi-Adad, King of the Universe, King of Assyria, Mother of Adad Nirari, King of the Universe, King of Assyria, Daughter-in-law of Shalmaneser, King of the Four Regions of the World.* The stele she built for herself carefully links her to every Assyrian king.

The Greek version of Sammuramat's story

THE SHEPHERD FINDS THE BABE SEMIRAMIS
From the Painting by E. Wallcousins

Hundreds of years later, the Greeks named her Semiramis. In the fifth century BC, the Greek physician and historian Ctesias writes a story about Semiramis in one of his books, *Persika*, that covers the "history" of Assyria and Babylon, none of which reconcile with the cuneiform evidence. According to his own account, Ctesias was taken as a prisoner of war by the Persians and served as a personal physician to the emperor and his family for seventeen years, where he gained the trust and confidence of the emperor's family—notably of Parysatis, the king's mother, and Statira, the king's wife, and these were the main sources of his work.

Most of the Assyrian monarchs in Ctesias' work *Persika* are mythical figures. Up until the eighteenth century, many historians turned to him for Assyrian history because he was thought to be the best source available. Then in the eighteenth century the discovery of the Assyrian king list tablets exposed that the royal lineage recorded by Ctesias was evidently false, like many of his other historical claims such as the stories of a race of people with only one leg or with feet so big they could be used as an umbrella. Yet Greek historian Diodorus Siculus (90-30 BCE) in his work *Historical Library*, written over a course of thirty years, drew on Ctesias's work, which no longer exists, even though Ctesias was ridiculed for inaccuracy by other ancient writers.

The story goes as follows:

Not far from the Syrian city of Ascalon is a large and deep lake full of fish. On its shore is a famous goddess, Derceto, who has the head of a woman and the body of a fish. Legend has it that Aphrodite, who was offended with this goddess, inspired in her a violent passion for a certain handsome Syrian youth among her votaries. Derceto gave herself to the Syrian and bore a daughter, but then, filled with shame because of her sinful deed, she killed her lover and abandoned the child in a rocky desert region, while as for herself, from shame and grief, she threw herself into the lake. Her body was changed into a fish.

A great multitude of doves had their nests where the baby girl was abandoned. The doves nurtured the baby in an astounding and miraculous manner, some keeping the baby warm on all sides by covering her with their wings while others brought her milk in their beak and fed her by putting the milk drop by drop between her lips. When the child was a year old and in need of solid nourishments, the doves supplied the child with nourishment by picking off cheese.

Now the keepers returned and saw that the cheeses had been nibbled about the edges. Astonished, they posted a lookout and discovered the infant, who was of surpassing beauty.

They brought the baby to the keeper of the royal herds, Simmas, and Simmas, being childless, gave every care to the rearing of the girl, raising her as his own daughter. He called her Semiramis, a name slightly altered from the word which, in the language of the Syrians, means "doves," birds all the inhabitants of Syria have continued to honor as goddesses since that time.

When Semiramis grew to the age of marriage, far surpassing all the other maidens in beauty, an officer named Onnes was sent from the king's court to inspect the royal herds. Upon arriving, he saw Semiramis and was captivated by her beauty. He earnestly entreated Simmas to give him the maiden in lawful marriage and took her off to Ninus, where he married her and begat two sons, Hyapates and Hydaspes. Because the other qualities of Semiramis matched the beauty of her countenance, her husband became completely enraptured by her, and since he would do nothing without her advice, he prospered in everything.

During this time King Ninus, now that he had completed the founding of the city which bore his name, undertook his campaign against the Bactrians, thus enrolling a great host of soldiers from all the negotiations under his sway. A fierce struggle then ensued in which the Bactrians put the Assyrians to flight and pursued them as far as the mountains which overlooked the field, killing about one hundred thousand of the enemy. But later, when the whole Assyrian force entered their country, the Bactrians, overpowered by the multitude of Assyrians, withdrew city by city, each group intending to defend its own homeland. And so Ninus easily subdued all the other cities, but because of Bactra's strength and the equipment for war which it contained, he was unable to take Bactra by storm.

Mesopotamian Goddesses

The siege proved to be a long affair, so Semiramis' husband, enamored with his wife and involved in the campaign with the king, sent for the woman. And she, endowed as she was with understanding, daring, and all the other qualities which contribute to distinction, seized the opportunity to display her native ability. First, she devised a garb which made it impossible to distinguish whether the wearer of it was a man or a woman. This dress was well adapted to her needs, especially for her travels in the heat, for protecting the color of her skin, and for providing her the convenience to do whatever she might wish to do.

When Semiramis arrived in Bactriana and observed the progress of the siege, she noted that it was on the plains and at positions which were easily assailed that attacks were being made, but no one had ever assaulted the acropolis because of its strong position. She also noted that its defender had left their posts there and were coming to the aid of those who were hard pressed on the walls below. Consequently, after taking with her the soldiers that were accustomed to clambering up rocky heights and making her way with them up through a certain difficult ravine, she seized a part of the acropolis and gave a signal to those who were besieging the wall down in the plain. Thereupon the defenders of the city, struck with terror at the size of the height, left the walls and abandoned all hope of saving themselves.

When the city had been taken in this way, the king, marveling at the ability of the woman, at first honored her with great gifts. Later, he became infatuated with her because of her beauty and tried to persuade her husband to yield her to him of his own accord, offering in return for this favor to give him his own daughter Sosanê to marry. But when the man took his offer with ill grace, Ninus threatened to put out his eyes unless he at once acceded to his commands. Onnes, partly out of fear of the king's threats and partly out of his passion for his wife, fell into a kind of frenzy and madness, put a rope about his neck, and hanged himself. Such, then, were the circumstances whereby Semiramis attained the position of queen.

Ninus secured the treasures of Bactra, which contained a great amount of both gold and silver, and after settling the affairs of Bactriana, disbanded his forces. After this he begat by Semiramis a son, Ninyas, and then died, leaving his wife as queen. Semiramis buried Ninus in the precinct of the palace and erected over his tomb a very large mound, nine stade high and ten wide, as Ctesias says. Consequently, since the city lay on a plain along the Euphrates, the mound was visible for a distance of many stade, like an acropolis; and this mound stands, they say, even to this day, though Ninus was razed to the ground by the Medes when they destroyed the empire of the Assyrians.

Semiramis, whose nature made her eager for great exploits and ambitious to surpass the fame of her predecessor on the throne, set her mind upon founding a city in Babylonia, and after securing the architects of all the world and skilled artisans and making all the other necessary preparations, she gathered together from her entire kingdom two million men to complete the work. Taking the Euphrates river into the center, she threw about the city a wall with great towers set at frequent intervals, the wall being three hundred and sixty stade in circumference, as Ctesias of Cnidus says, but according to the account of Cleitarchus and those who at a later time crossed into Asia with Alexander, it was actually three hundred and sixty-five stade. Later, it is said that it was her desire to make the number of stade the same as the days in the year.

Making baked bricks fast in bitumen, she built a wall with a height, as Ctesias says, of fifty fathoms, but, as some later writers have recorded, of fifty cubits, and wide enough for more than two chariots abreast to drive upon; and the towers numbered two hundred and fifty, their height and width corresponding to the massive scale of the wall.

Semiramis constructed a small number of towers. Since over a long distance the city was surrounded by swamps, she decided not to build towers along that space, the swamps offering a sufficient natural defense. And all along between the dwellings and the walls a road was left two plethra wide.

In order to expedite the building of these constructions she apportioned a stade to each of her friends, furnishing sufficient material for their task and directing them to complete their work within a year. And when they had finished these assignments with great speed she gratefully accepted their zeal, but she took for herself the construction of a bridge five stade long at the narrowest point of the river.

Semiramis also built two palaces on the very banks of the river, one at each end of the bridge. From both palaces, she intended to be able to look down over the entire city and to hold the keys, as it were, to its most important sections. And since the Euphrates River passed through the center of Babylon and flowed in a southerly direction, one palace faced the rising and the other the setting sun, and both had been constructed on a lavish scale.

On both the towers and the walls there were animal drawings of every kind, ingeniously executed by the use of colors as well as by the realistic imitation of the several types; and the whole had been made to represent a hunt, complete in every detail, of all sorts of wild animals. Among the animals, moreover, Semiramis had also been portrayed, on horseback and in the act of hurling a javelin at a leopard, and nearby was her husband Ninus, in the act of thrusting his spear into a lion at close quarters. In this wall she also set triple gates, two of which were of bronze and were opened by a mechanical device.

After this Semiramis picked out the lowest spot in Babylonia and built a square reservoir, which was three hundred stade long on each side; she built within seven days an underground passageway from one palace to the other; since the stream flowed above the passageway, Semiramis was able to go across from one palace to the other without passing over the river. At each end of the passageway, she also set bronze gates which stood until the time of the Persian rule.

After this she built in the center of the city a temple of Zeus, whom the Babylonians call Belus. In regards to this temple, the historians are at variance, and since time has caused the structure to fall into ruins, it is impossible to give the exact facts concerning it. But all agree that it was exceedingly high, and that in it the Chaldeans made their observations of the stars, whose risings and settings could be accurately observed because of the height of the structure.

The possessions of that great empire were later carried off as spoils by the kings of the Persians, while as for the palaces and the other buildings, time has either entirely effaced them or left them in ruins. In fact, merely a small part of Babylon itself is inhabited nowadays, and most of the area within its walls is used for agriculture.

Semiramis founded other cities along the Euphrates and Tigris rivers, in which she established trading places for the merchants who brought goods from Media, Paraetacenê, and all the neighboring regions. For the Euphrates and Tigris, the most notable, one may say, of all the rivers of Asia after the Nile and Ganges, have their sources in the mountains of Armenia and are 2500 stade apart at their origin, and after flowing through Media and Paraetacenê they enter Mesopotamia, which they enclose between them, thus giving this name to the country. After this they pass through Babylonia and empty into the Red Sea. Moreover, since they are great streams and traverse a spacious territory, they offer many advantages to men who follow a merchant trade; and it is due to this fact that the regions along their banks are filled with prosperous trading places which contribute greatly to the fame of Babylonia.

She traveled from city to city, planting parks and buildings, inscribing her name on monuments, satisfying her taste for luxury. She was unwilling, however, to contract a lawful marriage, being afraid that she might be deprived of her power. Instead, she chose the most handsome of soldiers to have sex with and next made all who slept with her disappear.

She visited Persia and every other country over which she ruled throughout Asia. Everywhere she cut through the mountains and the precipitous cliffs and constructed expensive roads, while on the plains she made mounds, sometimes constructing them as tombs for those of her generals who died, and sometimes founding cities on their tops. And it was also her custom, whenever she made camp, to build little mounds, upon which setting her tent she could look down upon all the encampment. As a consequence, many of the works she built throughout Asia remain to this day and are called Works of Semiramis.

Semiramis subdued Egypt, most of Libya and Ethiopia, and after putting in order the affairs of those lands, she returned with her force to Bactra in Asia. Given that she had great forces and had been at peace for some time, she became eager to achieve some brilliant exploit in war. Informed that the Indian nation was the largest one in the world and likewise possessed both the most extensive and the fairest country, she purposed to make a campaign into India.

Observing that her forces would be greatly inferior because they lacked elephants, Semiramis conceived the plan to make dummies that looked like these animals, in the hopes that the Indians would be struck with terror because of their belief that no elephants existed at all apart from those found in India.

Accordingly, she chose three-hundred-thousand black oxen and distributed their meat among her artisans and the men who had been assigned the task of making the figures, but the hides she sewed together and stuffed with straw, and thus made dummies, copying in every detail the natural appearance of these animals. Each dummy had within it a man to take care of it and a camel and, when it was moved by the latter, to those who saw it from a distance it looked like an actual animal. The artisans who were engaged in making these dummies for her worked at their task in a certain court which had been surrounded by a wall and had gates which were carefully guarded. In this manner, neither could one of the workers within pass out, nor could anyone from outside come in. This she did so no one from the outside might see what was taking place and that no report about the dummies might escape to the Indians.

When the boats and the beasts had been prepared in the two allotted years, on the third she summoned her forces from everywhere to Bactriana. The multitude of the army which was assembled, as Ctesias of Cnidus has recorded, was three million foot-soldiers, two-hundred-thousand cavalry, and one-hundred-thousand chariots. There were also men mounted on camels, carrying swords four cubits long, as many in number as the chariots. And river boats which could be taken apart she built to the number of two thousand, and she had collected camels to carry the vessels overland. Camels also bore the dummies of the elephants, and the soldiers, by bringing their horses up to these camels, taught them not to fear the savage nature of the beasts.

When Stabrobates, the king of the Indians, heard of the immensity of the forces mentioned and of the exceedingly great preparations which had been made for the war, he was anxious to surpass Semiramis in every respect. First of all, then, he made four thousand river boats out of reeds, for along its rivers and marshy places India produces a great abundance of reeds, so large in diameter that a man cannot easily put his arms about them; and it is said, furthermore, that ships built of these are exceedingly serviceable, since this wood does not rot. Moreover, he gave great care to the preparation of his arms and by visiting all India gathered a far greater force than that which had been collected by Semiramis. Additionally, holding a hunt of the wild elephants and multiplying many times the number already at his disposal, he fitted them all out splendidly with such things as would strike terror in war; and the consequence was that when they advanced to the attack, the multitude of them as well as the towers upon their backs made them appear like a thing beyond the power of human nature to understand.

When he had made all his preparations for the war he dispatched messengers to Semiramis, who was already on the road, accusing her of being the aggressor in the war although no one from his country had injured her. Then, in the course of his letter, after saying many slanderous things against her, like calling her a strumpet and calling upon the gods as witnesses, he threatened that he would crucify her after he defeated her. Semiramis, however, after reading his letter dismissed his statements with laughter and remarked, "It will be in deeds that the Indian will make trial of my valor."

She arrived with her force to the Indus River and found the boats of the enemy ready for battle. Hastily putting together her boats and manning them with her best marines, she joined battle on the river, while the foot-soldiers which were drawn up along the banks also participated eagerly in the contest. The struggle raged for a long time and both sides fought spiritedly, but finally Semiramis was victorious and destroyed about a thousand of the boats, taking more than a few men prisoners. Elated by her victory, she reduced to slavery the islands in the river and the cities on them and gathered more than one hundred thousand captives.

After these events the king of the Indians withdrew his force from the river, giving the appearance of retreating in fear, but he actually withdrew with the intention of enticing the enemy to cross the river. Thereupon Semiramis, now that her undertakings were as prosperous as she wished, spanned the river with a costly and large bridge, by means of which she got all her forces across; and then she left sixty thousand men to guard the pontoon bridge, while with the rest of her army she advanced in pursuit of the Indians, the dummy elephants leading the way so that the king's spies might report to the king the multitude of these animals in her army. Nor was she deceived in this hope; on the contrary, when those who had been dispatched to spy her out reported to the Indians the multitude of elephants among the enemy, they were all at a loss to discover from where such a multitude of beasts as accompanied her could have come. However, the deception did not remain a secret for long; for some of Semiramis' troops were caught neglecting their night watches in the camp, and these, in fear of the consequent punishment, deserted to the enemy and pointed out to them their mistake regarding the nature of the elephants. Encouraged by this information, the king of the Indians, after informing his army about the dummies, set his forces in array and turned about to face the Assyrians.

Semiramis likewise marshaled her forces, and as the two armies neared each other, Stabrobates, the king of the Indians, dispatched his cavalry and chariots far in advance of the main body. But the queen stoutly withstood the attack of the cavalry, and since the elephants which she had fabricated had been stationed at equal intervals in front of the main body of troops, it came about that the horses of the Indians shied at them. For whereas at a distance the dummies looked like the actual animals with which the horses of the Indians were acquainted and therefore charged upon them boldly enough, yet on nearer contact the odor which reached the horses was unfamiliar, and then the other differences, which taken all together were very great, threw them into utter confusion.

As a result, some of the Indians were thrown to the ground, while others, whence their horses would not obey the rein, were carried with their mounts hurriedly into the midst of the enemy. Then Semiramis, who was in the battle with a select band of soldiers, made skillful use of her advantage and put the Indians to flight.

Although those men fled toward the battle line, King Stabrobates, undismayed, advanced the ranks of his foot soldiers, keeping the elephants in front, while he himself, taking his position on the right wing and fighting from the most powerful of the beasts, charged in terrifying fashion upon the queen, whom chance had placed opposite him. Since the rest of the elephants followed his example, the army of Semiramis withstood but a short time the attack of the beasts; for the animals, by virtue of their extraordinary courage and the confidence which they felt in their power, easily destroyed everyone who tried to withstand them. Thus there was a great slaughter, which was achieved in various ways, some being trampled beneath their feet, others ripped up by their tusks, and a number tossed into the air by their trunks. A great multitude of corpses lay piled one upon the other. The danger aroused terrible alarm and fear in those who witnessed the sight. Afterward, not a man had the courage to hold his position any longer.

After the entire multitude turned into flight, the king of the Indians pressed his attack upon Semiramis herself. First he let fly an arrow and struck her on the arm, and then with his spear he pierced the back of the queen, but only with a glancing blow. Semiramis was not seriously injured and rode swiftly away, the pursuing beast being much inferior in speed. With everyone fleeing to the pontoon bridge and the great multitude forcing its way into a single narrow space, some of the queen's soldiers perished by being trampled upon by one another and by cavalry and foot soldiers being thrown together in unnatural confusion. When the Indians pressed hard upon them a violent crowding took place on the bridge because of their terror, so that many were pushed to either side of the bridge and fell into the river.

As for Semiramis, when the largest part of the survivors of the battle had found safety by putting the river behind them, she cut the fastenings which held the bridge together. When these were loosened the pontoon bridge, having been broken apart at many points and bearing great numbers of pursuing Indians, was carried down in haphazard fashion by the violence of the current and caused the death of many of the Indians, but for Semiramis it was the means of complete safety, the enemy now being prevented from crossing over against her.

The last events caused the king of the Indians to remain inactive, since heavenly omens appeared to him which his seers interpreted to mean that he must not cross the river. Semiramis, after exchanging prisoners, made her way back to Bactra with the loss of two-thirds of her force.

Sometime later her son Ninyas conspired against her through the agency of a certain eunuch. Remembering the prophecy given to her by Ammon, she did not punish the conspirator, but, on the contrary, after turning the kingdom over to him and commanding the governors to obey him, she at once disappeared, as if she were going to be translated to the gods as the oracle had predicted. Some, making a myth of it, say that she turned into a dove and flew off in the company of many birds which alighted on her dwelling, and this, they say, is the reason why the Assyrians worship the dove as a god, thus deifying Semiramis. Be that as it may, this woman, after having been queen over all Asia with the exception of India, passed away in the manner mentioned above, having lived sixty-two years and having reigned forty-two.

Such, then, is the account that Ctesias of Cnidus has given about Semiramis. But Athenaeus and certain other historians say that she was a comely courtesan and because of her beauty was loved by the king of the Assyrians, that at first she was accorded only a moderate acceptance in the palace, but later, when she had been proclaimed a lawful wife, she persuaded the king to yield the royal privileges to her for a period of five days. Semiramis, upon receiving the scepter and the regal dress, on the first day held a high festival and gave a magnificent banquet, at which she persuaded the commanders of the military forces and all the greatest dignitaries to cooperate with her; and on the second day, while the people and the most notable citizens were paying her their respects as queen, she arrested her husband and put him in prison; and since she was by nature a woman of great designs and bold as well, she seized the throne and remained queen until old age. She accomplished many great things.

Such, then, are the conflicting accounts which may be found in historian accounts regarding the career of Semiramis.

The following is the Armenian account of Semiramis.

Once upon a time, there lived a woman named Semiramis, the queen of Nineveh. Her husband Ninus begins to detest her for her infidelity and leaves his country to go to Crete. Semiramis then hears about the fame of the handsome Armenian king Ara Geghetsik. The Armenians are an ancient people whose home lies in the highlands surrounding the biblical mountains of Ararat, upon which tradition tells us Noah's ark came to rest after the Flood. The Armenian Highlands were an integral part of ancient Mediterranean and Mesopotamian civilization and their neighbors included the Hittites, Israelites, Assyrians, Babylonians, Medes, Persians, and Greeks.

During the time of Semiramis' tale, Ara had succeeded his father Aram as ruler of the land of his forefathers. He was a very handsome young prince and Ninus, Semiramis' husband, did not interfere with his rule. But Semiramis, with her husband now gone, lusts after Ara's image and asks him to come to Nineveh to marry her. But he was already married to his devoted wife Nvard, so he refuses. Semiramis sends ambassadors, offers him the throne and showers him with gifts and proposals of marriage. Ara continues to reject her advances. Furious, she gathers her army and marches toward Armenia, where a battle ensues.

Semiramis orders her commanders to capture Ara alive, but one of her sons beats and kills him. His body is found on the battlefield among the other slain soldiers. To pacify the Armenians who want to continue to fight to avenge his death, Semiramis says, "I have prayed to the gods to lick his wounds and heal him. Ara will revive."

A sorceress, Semiramis believes her powers will actually revive him and she frantically tries to do just that. When she sees his corpse decaying, she becomes distraught and has her servants bury it in a deep grave. She then dresses one of her warriors as Ara, comes before the Armenians and says, "Licking his wounds the gods gave life back to Ara, thus fulfilling our deepest desires. Since they have bestowed on us happiness, we should exalt them more than before."

She has a new statue erected to the gods and offers them many sacrifices for saving Ara. The people believe that Ara revived so they relinquish the idea of waging a battle against her. Semiramis names his twelve-year-old son, Karthos, after him to eternalize her love for him, and then she makes him ruler of Armenia despite his young age.

On her way back to Ninevah, the delighted Assyrian queen travels by the eastern shores of Lake Van. Struck by the beauty and charm of the Plain of Ayrarat, its cool air and pure waters, she brings thousands of workers and numerous architects to build a magnificent summer palace on the rocky cliffs nearby. She remains in that city, and on the hard face of the rock, inscribes many texts and memorials in cuneiform scripts. She appoints as her representative in Assyria and Nineveh, Zoroaster, the religious leader and oracle of the Medes, and as such he rules the country well for a long time.

When her children grow up, they want to seize Semiramis' throne and confiscate her treasure. They openly accuse her of disgraceful deeds. Enraged, she has all of her children killed with the exception of her youngest son, Ninyas, and leaves her throne and treasures to her lovers instead. Zoroaster tries to seize the throne, and in the subsequent battle defeats Semiramis, so she flees to Armenia. Her son Ninyas grabs this opportunity to kill her, avenging his siblings, and becomes the ruler of the kingdom. Ara's son also dies during the battle, leaving a son named Anushavan.

Another version of the story of Ara and Semiramis is tied to the mountain that has Ara's name (Arai Lehr). In this story, Ara is cast upon the mountain by Semiramis after he rejects her advances. Semiramis, skilled in black magic, conjured the forces of the night to throw him into the void, and when he lands, his body sinks onto the top of the mount, giving it its present silhouette. Another tale says that when Ara dies, Semiramis has him buried at the foot of the mountain. His spirit rises and forms the top of the mountain into his sleeping likeness. The top of the mountain resembles the contour of a man's face. The ancient Armenian city Shamiramagerd means "created by Semiramis."

Armenian tradition portrays Semiramis as a home-wrecker and harlot.

Over a thousand years later…

Over a thousand years later, yet another story comes up about Semiramis. This time it's by Alexander Hislop, a Free Church of Scotland minister, known for his criticism of the Roman Catholic Church. Hislop wrote several books, his most famous one being *The Two Babylons: Papal Worship Proved to be the Worship of Nimrod and His Wife*.

The book was published in 1853, and the basic idea discussed in the book is that the pagan religion of ancient Babylon has continued to our modern day, disguised as the Roman Catholic Church, as prophesied in the Book of Revelation as "Mystery Babylon the Great." Hislop's idea of two Babylons, one ancient and one modern, was taken to be so factual that he became known as an authority in paganism until it was discovered that he didn't at all offer a reliable historical account but instead had pieced together ancient myths embroidered with his own inventions. Even most of his footnote references did not support his claims.

Hislop links a Chaldean Semiramis to the whore of Babylon although she's never mentioned in the Bible. According to him, she is the mother of Nimrod, the great-grandson of Noah who becomes king of Babylon and creates the worship of idolatry. Nimrod is a mighty hunter, described in Genesis 10:8-12 as "the first on earth to be a mighty man." In the Bible, Nimrod is the first human to rebel against God after the Flood. In Hislop's account, Nimrod is a big, ugly, deformed black man.

Nimrod marries his mother Semiramis, a beautiful white woman with blond hair and blue eyes. She invents polytheism and, with it, goddess worship, a system based on the stars, and so therefore she becomes associated with Ishtar, the original Queen of Heaven. Nimrod's uncle Shem kills Nimrod for his sins of idolatry, chopping his body and scattering the pieces all around as a lesson to the people. But the effort to end Nimrod's paganism fails because his Semiramis, his mother/wife/widow, continues the religion.

After Nimrod's death in 2167 BC, Semiramis declares that she was visited by the spirit of Nimrod, who left her pregnant through a miraculous conception. She gives birth to the Akkadian deity Tammuz, a god of vegetation, as well as a life-death-rebirth deity because, she says, he is the reincarnation of Nimrod. She promotes the belief that Nimrod was a god, thus she's the "Mother of God"—the title given to the Virgin Mary by the Eastern and Oriental Orthodox, Catholic, Anglican, and Lutheran churches who believe that since Jesus was God, then Mary is the "Mother of God."

With a father, mother, and son deified, a trinity was formed for Semiramis, and Semiramis and her son were worshiped as "Madonna and child." As the generations passed, they were worshipped under other names in different countries and languages: Isis and Osiris in Egypt, Venus and Adonis in Greece, and Ushas and Vishnu in Hinduism. Hislop believes that Roman

Catholicism is a modified form of Babylonian religion and that they adapted the mother/son worship into their veneration of Mary, that Catholics worship Nimrod, not Jesus, and pray to his mother Semiramis, not Mary. He said that the Babylonians baptized in water, believing it had virtue because Nimrod and Semiramis suffered for them in water.

Hislop's book *The Two Babylons* claims that modern Catholic holidays, including Christmas and Easter, are actually pagan festivals established by Semiramis and that the customs associated with them are pagan rituals, crediting Semiramis for saying that, after Nimrod's death (c. 2167 BC), she promotes the belief that he was a god. She claims that a full-grown evergreen tree sprung out of the roots of a dead tree stump, symbolizing the springing forth of new life for Nimrod. On the anniversary of his birth, which fell on the winter solstice at the end of December, she says that Nimrod would visit the evergreen tree and leave gifts under it. During the time between Babel and Christ, pagans developed the belief that the days grew shorter in early winter because their sun-god was leaving them. When they saw the length of the day increasing, they had a celebration known as *Saturnalia*, named after Saturn, another name for Nimrod. Ancient people celebrated the death and rebirth of the sun.

In the end, Hislop writes, one of Semiramis' sons kills her by chopping off her head.

While there's no mention of Semiramis in the Bible and no mention of Nimrod in Babylonian cuneiforms, those who believe that she was Nimrod's mother and wife have reached the following conclusion by this theory that has been published word-for-word on numerous websites and in numerous books:

The initial element "sammur" when translated into Hebrew becomes "Shinar," the biblical name for lower Mesopotamia, and is the word from which we derive "Sumeria." This one tarnished woman had such a lasting impact upon world history that not only do we call by her name the land from which civilization flowed, but God himself through the sacred writer has let us know that its distinguishing characteristic was that it was "the Land of Shinar," or Semiramis. Very little has come down to us through the millennia concerning Semiramis' rise to power, but it is safe to assume that it was initially upon Nimrod's coattails that she rode, although later in life as well as throughout history her influence overwhelmingly obscured that of her husband. Of course, it would not do to have an ex-harlot upon the throne, so the "polite fiction" was invented that she was a virgin sprung from the sea at Nimrod's landing, and hence a suitable bride for the emperor, thus the title Semiramis which has totally obscured her original name.

The lies we've been told through the ages about an ancient sophisticated civilization, especially as it pertains toward women, is so profound that many people have held onto these lies with dear life even though the lies were not founded on any evidence and have perpetuated a divide-and-conquer mentality and taken us backwards. People are so locked into certain belief systems that rather than learn from that world's practical teachings, they cannot stop arguing with each other, going as far as killing to prove that they are the righteous messenger who God has given commands to. They don't investigate. They don't question the highly questionable stories which don't match with the historic science and artifacts that they are based on.

These lies have been brought on by the ignorance of modern man. These lies have decimated and removed people from their culture and their history. These lies have weakened peoples' connection to who they are, taking away the memory of their true power. When that happens, it's difficult for us to feel worthy, because we've forgotten why we've come to this earth to begin with. Reestablishing the truth about our spiritual origin is truly needed in today's world, where people have fallen off balance and hurt themselves and others as a result.

How do we return to a sophisticated and refined society? If we understand our history and how we got here, then we can better understand how to get where we want to go. We can have the courage to take responsibility for our lives instead of blaming others, including evil spirits. Some religions accuse Semiramis' and the biblical Jezebel's wicked spirits for sneaking into today's church in various ways, including through the Virgin Mary, and creating all sorts of dishevel.

The more we research, the more we realize what people claim is history is not always the case. Rather, it's simply a story written by someone, whoever this person(s) may be. For instance, in the case of Semiramis, several authors wrote stories about her that had no historical evidence and have been proven to be false, but readers who wanted to believe that those stories are true have embraced them as such and have used them as propaganda to further their agenda.

Authors are human and not gods. The written word is written by humans, humans who have their own interpretation of God and the world and who usually have their own agendas and in many cases are on a power trip. It's important to know who the author is, to inquire, analyze his or her ideas, and not simply accept it as the word of God. As Alexander Hislop's first line in the introduction of his book states, "There is this great difference between the works of men and the works of God." He considered his works to be that of God, and just because he said so, people believed it. Some still do, even though his hypothesis has been strongly debunked.

For thousands of years, male writers have described powerful female leaders as cunning, ruthless, promiscuous, and reprehensible women. They characterized them as evil and made their names synonymous with idolaters, prostitutes, and sorcerers. With these labels, they used fear to keep us from ever wanting to know who these women really were in history. Unless she was submissive and a martyr, flattering descriptions didn't accompany her name the way it did her male counterparts whose brutal strengths were considered legendary and godly. A man fighting for what he believed in was called courageous, loyal, his name elevated to a prophet. A woman with similar desires and courage received the opposite treatment.

What important family story was handed down to you through oral tradition? Have you ever asked yourself if it's accurate? Who were the heroes and heroines and who were the villains? Have you ever looked at the story from each character's perspective? Have you wondered how this story has affected who you are today? If not, take the time to do so now. Write down the different parts of this family story, the beginning, middle, and end. Put yourself in each character's shoes, imagining their circumstances and why they made the decisions they made. Reflect on how their story impacted or parallels your story. Remember to include the good qualities and the not-so good qualities you inherited from it. Then decide what story you want to leave for those closest to you. Give birth to that story by becoming its author, like Enehduanna signing the end with your name.

Chapter 13

Asherah
The Mother Goddess

Emerging in Mesopotamia about 2000 BCE as the Amorite goddess Ashratu, she was the wife of Amurru, chief deity of early Babylon. This goddess later migrates to Caanite as Asherah, the wife of El, Creator of Earth. El eventually becomes assimilated to Yahweh. Yahweh is non-gendered and correctly translated means "the One who is" or "I am." All modern English translations render it as "Lord." So Asherah becomes known as the wife of God, thus the Grand Mother of Jews, Christians and Muslims. All of Mesopotamian mythology had the male/female pair. It was the natural order of that time and place.

Asherah's connection to Yahweh is both in the Bible, where she's mentioned about forty times, and an eight century BC inscription on pottery found in the Sinai desert at a site called Kuntillet Airud. The inscription is a prayer that asks for a blessing from Yahweh and his Asherah. Ancient texts, amulets, and figurines reveal that Asherah was a powerful fertility goddess, worshipped in Yahweh's Temple in Jerusalem in a garden where the serpent was her sacred totem. Female personnel wove ritual textiles for her.

Hammurabi called her "Bride of the Lord of Heavens." Many titles are attributed to Asherah, but mostly "The Mother Goddess," "Tree of Life," "Lady Who Treads on the Sea," and "Goddess of the Sea," starting a long tradition of association between the feminine and the sea/water. She is said to have birthed at least seventy sons with El. El had two wives, but only Asherah nursed the newly born gods. Her powers and her presence were invoked not only during planting time but also during childbirth. She's mentioned in the childbirth prayer written thousands of years ago in Phoenician, which is very similar to biblical Hebrew.

In *The Epic of Baal*, Baal, Lord of the Earth, desires the kingship of the gods and he contends with Prince Yam, the son of El. El decides the case in favor of his son and gives the kingship to Prince Yam. Yam rules the gods with an iron fist, causing them to labor and toil under his reign, so the gods turn to their mother, Asherah, crying for help. They convince her to confront Yam, to intercede in their behalf.

Asherah obliges and goes into the presence of Prince

Yam, begs him to release his grip upon the gods, her sons. Yam declines her request. She offers favors to the tyrant, none of which soften his heart. Finally, Asherah, who loves her children, offers herself to the God of the Sea. She offers her own body to the Lord of Rivers. Yam agrees to this and Asherah returns home to the court of El, steps before the Divine Council, and speaks about her plan to the gods, her children.

Baal is infuriated by her speech, angered at the gods who would allow such a plot. He swears to the gods that he would destroy Prince Yam and lay to rest his tyranny. And that's exactly what he does. He kills Yam. Baal then tries to attain a palace equivalent in splendor to those of other gods. He sends Kothar to persuade Asherah to intervene with her husband El, the head of the pantheon, to approve the construction of a palace. Kothar thus goes to the Lady of the Sea and offers her gifts.

When reading *The Epic of Baal*, one sees how Asherah, like Jesus, rode a donkey, a symbol of peace, on her triumphant journey since horses were mostly used for wars. Yet in the East, people of the highest rank rode a donkey, such as Prophet Abraham, and decorated its saddle and harness as richly as those of the horse.

The Epic of Baal

>They besought Lady Asherah of the Sea.
>Yea entreated the Creatress of the Gods.
>And Lady Asherah of the Sea replied:
>"How can Ye beseech Lady Asherah of the Sea,
>Yea entreat the Creatress of the Gods?
>Have Ye besought The Bull, God of Mercy,

Or entreated the Creator of Creatures?
And the Virgin Anath replied:
"We do beseech Lady Asherah of the Sea.
We entreat the Creatress of Gods.
The Gods eat and drink,
And those that suck the breast quaff
With a keen knife
A slice of fatling.
They drink wine from a goblet,
From a cup of gold, the blood of vines."

Asherah of the Sea declares:
"Saddle an ass,
Hitch a donkey!
Put on a harness of silver,
Trappings of gold.
Prepare the harness of My jennies!

Qadish-u-Amrar hearkens.
He saddles an ass
Hitches a donkey.
Put on a harness of silver,
Trappings of gold.
Prepares the harness of Her jennies!
Qadish-u-Amrar embraces;
He sets Asherah on the back of the ass,
On the beautiful back of the donkey.
Qadish begins to light the way,
Even Amrar like a star.
Forward goes the Virgin Anath,
And Baal departs for the heights of Saphon.

Then She sets face toward El,
At the sources of the Two Rivers,
In the midst of the streams of the Two Deeps.
She enters the abode of El,
And comes into the domicile of the King, Father Shunem.
At the feet of El She bows and falls,
She prostrates Herself and honors Him.

As soon as El sees Her,
He cracks a smile and laughs.
His feet He sets on the footstool,
And twiddles His fingers.
He lifts His voice
And shouts:
"Why has Lady Asherah of the Sea come?
Why came the Creatress of Gods?
Art Thou hungry?
Then have a morsel!
Or art Thou thirsty?
Then have a drink!
Eat!
Or drink!
Eat bread from the tables!
Drink wine from the goblets!
From a cup of gold, the blood of vines!
If the love of El moves Thee,
Yea the affection of The Bull arouses Thee!"

And Lady Asherah of the Sea replies:
"Thy word, El, is wise;
Thou art wise unto eternity;

Mesopotamian Goddesses

Lucky life is Thy word.
Our king is Aliyan Baal,
Out judge, and none is above Him.
Let both of Us drain His chalice;
Both of Us drain His cup!"

Loudly Bull-El, Her father, shouts,
King El who brought Her into being;
There shout Asherah and Her sons,
The Goddess and the band of Her brood:
"Lo there is no house unto Baal like the Gods.
Not a court like the sons of Asherah:
The dwelling of El,
The shelter of His sons.
The dwelling of Lady Asherah of the Sea,
The dwelling of the renowned brides.
The dwelling of Pidray, girl of Light.
The shelter of Tallay, girl of rain.
The dwelling of Arsay, girl of Yaabdar."

And the God of Mercy replied:
"Am I to act as a lackey of Asherah?
Am I to act like the holder of a trowel?
If the handmaid of Asherah will make the bricks
A house shall be built for Baal like the Gods.
Yea a court like the sons of Asherah."

And Lady Asherah of the Sea replied:
"Thou art great, O El,
Thou are verily wise!
The gray of Thy beard hath verily instructed Thee!

Here are pectorals of gold for Thy breast.

Lo, also it is the time of His rain.
Baal sets the season,
And gives forth His voice from the clouds.
He flashes lightning to the earth.
As a house of cedars let Him complete it,
Or a house of bricks let Him erect it!
Let it be told to Aliyan Baal:
'The mountains will bring Thee much silver.
The hills, the choicest of gold;
The mines will bring Thee precious stones,
And build a house of silver and gold.
A house of lapis gems!'"

The Virgin Anath rejoices.
She jumps with the feet
And leaves the earth.
Then She sets face toward the Lord of Saphon's crest
By the thousand acres,
Yea the myriad hectares.
The Virgin Anath laughs.
She lifts Her voice
And shouts:
"Be informed, Baal!
Thy news I bring!
A house shall be built for Thee as for Thy brothers,
Even as a court as for Thy kin!
The mountains will bring Thee much silver.
The hills, the choicest of gold;
The mines will bring Thee precious stones,

And build a house of silver and gold.
A house of lapis gems!"
Aliyan Baal rejoices.

Archeological evidence shows that the people who became Israelites were mostly native Canaanites who settled in the hills of what is now the West Bank. Small but significant groups also migrated there from the south in and around the Arabah Valley in Sinai. That's where at around 850 BC, Yahweh worship seems to have originated as El and Yahweh became mixed together. Asherah came to be known as Yahweh's wife.

She was part of Israelite religion, with an Asherah pole standing in front of Solomon's Temple for most of its existence, as well as in Yahweh's sanctuary in Samaria. Originally in the ancient Near East, the goddess was associated with and had jurisdiction over vegetation and life and set up a sacred garden sanctuary. Garden sanctuaries of gods and kings evolved later, when religion became more patriarchal, sky gods came to dominate, and goddesses were substantially devalued. In the Eden story, Yahweh is both creating the garden (i.e. life) and in charge of it.

In harmony with the seasons, trees represent the life source and epitomize the creation, renewal, and re-renewal of life. Thus, they are associated with the Earth/Mother Goddess. They're also believed to connect with the divine realms of both the underworld and the heavens. In Palestine, sacred trees were venerated in sanctuaries known as "high places" as means of accessing and experiencing divinity, principally the goddess Asherah. The divinity of the male deity was accessed through vertical stone pillars, like the one set up by Jacob at Bethel.

In the Eden story, the two sacred trees of knowledge

of good and evil refer to this historical role of sacred trees. However, in the newer version, Yahweh not only creates the tree, but commands Adam and Eve not to partake of the tree. He begins a new message for future generations not to venerate sacred trees in the traditional fashion. Israelites set up a tree or a stylized tree next to altars of the lord from the earliest times. These were sometimes called groves even if it was one tree or a poll. Genesis 21:33 says, "And Abraham planted a grove in Beersheba, and called there on the name of the Lord, the everlasting God." Although it doesn't specifically mention Asherah, some say that since Asherah is translated as grove, this was uttered in her honor because it uses the phrase used in her worship.

Many object to this but not William Smith, who says of this word as it relates to Genesis 21:33, "Pliny expressly tells us, trees were the first temples; and from the earliest times groves are mentioned in connection with religious worship...The groves were generally found connected with temples, and often had the right of affording an asylum."

Not only did Abraham plant a grove for Asherah, Moses represented her in the tabernacle by the visual Menorah. The tabernacle Menorah, the seven branched candlestick of Jewish life and ritual, is shaped like a flowering almond tree and that of the moriah plant. The almond tree is the first of its kind to blossom in Israel and many scholars have considered the tabernacle Menorah to represent the tree of life, thus Asherah. From the time of Solomon, about 1015 BC, a stylized tree or poll was set up or symbolically planted in Solomon's temple, representing Asherah. After Solomon, various kings removed and restored the Asherah from the temple in turn, but it stood there for 213 years of the temple's existence before it was destroyed by the invading Babylonians. The Old Testament was written during the Babylonian Exile.

Around about 850 BC, Alijah confronts Ahab, accusing him of not obeying the Lord's commands by going after the Baals. He says, "Now tell all Israel to meet me at Mount Carmel. And bring the 450 prophets of Baal and the 400 prophets of Asherah, who eat at Jezebel's table." Jezebel was Ahab's wife.

Everyone showed up and Elijah said to the people, "I am the only prophet of the Lord here, but there are 450 prophets of Baal. Bring two bulls. Let the prophets of Baal choose one bull and kill it and cut it into pieces. Then let them put the meat on the wood, but they are not to set fire to it. I will prepare the other bull, putting the meat on the wood but not setting fire to it. You prophets of Baal, pray to your god, and I will pray to the Lord. The god who answers by setting fire to his wood is the true God."

Baal and his prophets did everything in their power to get a fire to start over the bull but nothing happened. However, the fire from the Lord came down and burned Elijah's fire and when all the people saw this, they fell to the ground, crying, "The Lord is God! The Lord is God!"

Then Elijah said, "Capture the prophets of Baal! Don't let any of them run away!" The people captured all the prophets. Then Elijah led them down to the Kishon Valley, where he killed them. But evidently, he left the prophets of Asherah unharmed. Elijah is credited with performing sixteen miracles, including being the first prophet in the Bible to raise the dead.

Asherah was venerated from the earliest time of Israel. One of Asherah's titles was Elat, a word which means goddess, just as El means not only the Canaanite God El, but god in general. The word Elat is translated in the Bible as terebinth, a large shade tree found in Israel. It seems that no prophet before 850 BC condemned the worship of Asherah. About 720 BC, King Hezekiah removed from the temple the Nehushtan, the brass serpent that Moses had set up to heal the people of the deserts. He removed the high places, broke down the pillars, and cut down the sacred poll, Asherah. He forbade the worship of Yahweh at the traditional hilltop shrines or anywhere else outside the temple. In those days, people made offerings to these places and burned incense to it. Here the serpent and the tree were being worshiped together.

About 640 BC, King Josiah (Jeremiah) and the Deuteronomist radically changed Israeli religion. They opposed the idea of a "Son of God" and tried to remove any remaining difference between El and Yahweh, merging them into one. They didn't believe in ongoing revelation and opposed the teaching that there is atonement. They changed the rituals of the temple on the day of Yom Kappur, also known as the Day of Atonement. Along with this, they oppressed and vilified Asherah from the temple, burned it, beat it to dust, and scattered it on common graves. Shortly thereafter, Jeremiah began to preach and denounced the worship of Asherah, at least as an idol.

Several hundred Asherah figurines from this same time have been found in a cave not a hundred yards from the temple. They portray a woman often nursing the divine child from the waist up and a tree trunk from the waist down, demonstrating Asherah's continuous association with the tree of life. Other artifacts depict Asherah naked, holding vegetative stalks like lotus blossoms or vines, signifying the providing of blessings to the people of the land. As a naked goddess, she was an expression of the procreative, the nurturing power of the female. Despite

Mesopotamian Goddesses

Josiah's efforts, her worship, which encompassed thirteen historical areas, continued.

The fall of Jerusalem marks the end of the worship of Asherah. In the Babylonian captivity, she was literally erased from mainstream Judaism. While some traces remained even after Deuteronomist reforms, little remains in the Bible as we have it today of her nature and character. Many teachings suppressed by the Deuteronomist reappear in the Christian church. Interestingly, the apostle John brings back the images of the tree of life beside the throne of god, a Holy of Holies and also the waters of life.

Asherah was not only acquainted with the tree of life but also with wisdom—a word which, in the Bible is personified as a woman. In English, the word *wisdom* is grammatically neutral, but in Hebrew it's *chokmoth*, feminine. A compilation of Hebrew writing called the Book of Wisdom is composed of the biblical books of Job, Psalms, Proverbs, Ecclesiastes, and Song of Solomon. Proverbs illustrates Wisdom performing activities that are usually associated with a woman, such as preparing a meal in Proverbs 9:2, 5. Understanding this connection of wisdom with Asherah puts many verses in a different light and reveals some of what the Hebrews thought about the goddess Asherah.

The Call of Wisdom

[20] Wisdom cries aloud in the street,
in the markets she raises her voice;
[21] at the head of the noisy streets she cries out;
at the entrance of the city gates she speaks:
[22] "How long, O simple ones, will you love being simple?
How long will scoffers delight in their scoffing

and fools hate knowledge?
²³ If you turn at my reproof,
behold, I will pour out my spirit to you;
I will make my words known to you.
²⁴ Because I have called and you refused to listen,
have stretched out my hand and no one has heeded,
²⁵ because you have ignored all my counsel
and would have none of my reproof,
²⁶ I also will laugh at your calamity;
I will mock when terror strikes you,
²⁷ when terror strikes you like a storm
and your calamity comes like a whirlwind,
when distress and anguish come upon you.
²⁸ Then they will call upon me, but I will not answer;
they will seek me diligently but will not find me.
²⁹ Because they hated knowledge
and did not choose the fear of the Lord,
³⁰ would have none of my counsel
and despised all my reproof,
³¹ therefore they shall eat the fruit of their way,
and have their fill of their own devices.
³² For the simple are killed by their turning away,
and the complacency of fools destroys them;
³³ but whoever listens to me will dwell secure
and will be at ease, without dread of disaster."

Wisdom - Mosiah 8:20, 21

O how marvelous are the works of the Lord, and how long doth he suffer with his people; yea, and how blind and impenetrable are the understandings of the children of men; for they will not seek wisdom, neither do they desire that she should rule over them! Yea, they are as a wild flock which fleeth from the shepherd, and scattereth, and are driven, and are devoured by the beasts of the forest.

Proverbs 3:13 - 26
[13] Blessed are those who find wisdom,
those who gain understanding,
[14] for she is more profitable than silver
and yields better returns than gold.
[15] She is more precious than rubies;
nothing you desire can compare with her.
[16] Long life is in her right hand;
in her left hand are riches and honor.
[17] Her ways are pleasant ways,
and all her paths are peace.
[18] She is a tree of life to those who take hold of her;
those who hold her fast will be blessed.
[19] By wisdom the Lord laid the earth's foundations,
by understanding he set the heavens in place;
[20] by his knowledge the watery depths were divided,
and the clouds let drop the dew.
[21] My son, do not let wisdom and understanding
out of your sight,
preserve sound judgment and discretion;
[22] they will be life for you,
an ornament to grace your neck.
[23] Then you will go on your way in safety,
and your foot will not stumble.
[24] When you lie down, you will not be afraid;
when you lie down, your sleep will be sweet.
[25] Have no fear of sudden disaster

or of the ruin that overtakes the wicked,
²⁶ for the Lord will be at your side
and will keep your foot from being snared.

Proverbs 4:5—4:9
⁵ Get wisdom, get understanding;
do not forget my words or turn away from them.
⁶ Do not forsake wisdom, and she will protect you;
love her, and she will watch over you.
⁷ The beginning of wisdom is this: Get wisdom.
Though it cost all you have, get understanding.
⁸ Cherish her, and she will exalt you;
embrace her, and she will honor you.
⁹ She will give you a garland to grace your head
and present you with a glorious crown."

The early prophets did not oppose Asherah's worship yet evidently, during the rise of patriarchy and monotheism, she was viewed as a threat. The writers of the Bible edited her out but not entirely. She's mentioned some forty times, always in a negative and hostile way. Many of her purposes and tasks are absorbed by Yahweh. The name of the goddess Tannit, the Phoenician version of Asherah, means "Serpent Lady," and she had the epithet "Lady Hawat," meaning "Lady of Life," which is derived from the same Canaaite word as Eve's name, Hawwa.

In the story of Eden, the serpent's posture when talking with Even is upright. Yahweh curses the serpent and flattens its posture. As a result, he is victorious over the serpent and chaos and, by implication, the goddess. Eve is punished by having to give birth in pain whereas goddesses in the ancient Near East gave birth painlessly. Further, in Genesis 4:1, Eve needs Yahweh's help to become fertile and conceive, a reversal of the goddess' power and function. Indeed, Eve is even created from Adam! Adam's only fault was "listening" to Eve to attain divine qualities. Here the Yahwist may be alluding to goddess veneration, saying not to worship her. This seems to be one reason for the punishment of woman's subjugation to man in Genesis 3:16.

By the end of the story, Yahweh is supreme and in control of all divine powers and functions formerly in the hands of the goddess, and Canaanite religion in general has been discredited. Yahweh is in charge of the garden, formerly the goddess' province, from which chaos has been removed. Sacred tree veneration has been prohibited and discredited while Yahweh appropriates and identifies himself with the tree of life. In Hosea 14:8, Yahweh claims, "I am like an evergreen cypress, from me comes your fruit."

The serpent has been vanquished, flattened, and deprived of divine qualities and thus is not worthy of veneration, and antagonism has been established between snakes and humans. The goddess has been discredited, rendered powerless, and is eliminated from the picture and sent into oblivion. Despite her association with Yahweh in extra-biblical sources, Yahweh in the Bible commands the destruction of her shrines so as to maintain purity of worship to Yahweh Himself, alone. He wanted everything to himself. So he divorces her.

In the Old Testament, the Book of Hosea, we learn that a woman, in this case Gomer, Hosea's wife, was free to marry, raise children, and continue to make love to other men at the temple, dressing in all her finery to do so. Even in these biblical accounts, which were obviously written to demean and debase her actions, the description revealed that she took part in the sexual customs of her own free will and that she viewed them not as an obligatory or compulsory duty but as pleasant occasions, rather like festive parties. This situation was clearly unacceptable to the men who espoused the patrilineal Hebrew system, as Hosea did, but it does reveal that for those who belonged to other religious systems it was quite typical behavior.

For thousands of years these sexual customs had been accepted as natural among the people of the Near and Middle East. They may have permitted and even encouraged matrilineal descent patterns and a female-kinship system to survive. Inherent within the very practice of the sexual customs was the lack of concern for the paternity of children—and it is only with a certain knowledge of paternity that a patrilineal system can be maintained.

The first few sections of the Book of Hosea most clearly depict the outrage of the Hebrew man with the wife who refused to be his private property. First we read that Yahweh told Hosea, "Take yourself a wife of harlotry and have children of harlotry, for the land commits great harlotry by forsaking the Lord." Hosea then spoke to his daughter of the "whoredom" and "lewdness" of her mother Gomer, who was apparently a sacred woman of the temple. Later Gomer was told to put away her harlotry and adultery, to which she defiantly replied, "I will go after my lovers." In response to this rebellion the male deity threatened to thwart her activities until such time as she would finally say in desperation, "I will go and return to my first husband."

It is not clear whether these were intended to be the words of Hosea or Yahweh, for they are initially presented as the words of Hosea to his wife, but then we read, "I will put an end to all her rejoicing, her feasts, her new moons, her Sabbaths and all her solemn festivals. I mean to make her pay for all the days when she offered burnt offerings to the Baals and decked herself with rings and necklaces to court her lovers, forgetting me. It is Yahweh who is speaking." Hosea then goes on to say. "Your daughters play the harlot and your brides commit adultery for the men go aside with harlots and sacrifice with cult prostitutes."

The husband, Hosea, so totally identified himself with the male deity that his words became the words of Yahweh. In the new religion not only the priests, but all men, were to be considered as direct messengers of the Lord, not merely in Church but in the privacy of a woman's kitchen or even in her bed.

Hosea 2
2 "Rebuke your mother, rebuke her,
for she is not my wife,
and I am not her husband.
Let her remove the adulterous look from her face
and the unfaithfulness from between her breasts.
3 Otherwise I will strip her naked
and make her as bare as on the day she was born;
I will make her like a desert,
turn her into a parched land,
and slay her with thirst.
4 I will not show my love to her children,
because they are the children of adultery.
5 Their mother has been unfaithful
and has conceived them in disgrace.
She said, 'I will go after my lovers,
who give me my food and my water,
my wool and my linen, my olive oil and my drink.'
6 Therefore I will block her path with thorn bushes;
I will wall her in so that she cannot find her way.

⁷ She will chase after her lovers but not catch them;
she will look for them but not find them.
Then she will say,
'I will go back to my husband as at first,
for then I was better off than now.'
⁸ She has not acknowledged that I was the one
who gave her the grain, the new wine and oil,
who lavished on her the silver and gold—
which they used for Baal.
⁹ "Therefore I will take away my grain when it ripens,
and my new wine when it is ready.
I will take back my wool and my linen,
intended to cover her naked body.
¹⁰ So now I will expose her lewdness
before the eyes of her lovers;
no one will take her out of my hands.
¹¹ I will stop all her celebrations:
her yearly festivals, her New Moons,
her Sabbath days—all her appointed festivals.
¹² I will ruin her vines and her fig trees,
which she said were her pay from her lovers;
I will make them a thicket,
and wild animals will devour them.
¹³ I will punish her for the days
she burned incense to the Baals;
she decked herself with rings and jewelry,
and went after her lovers,
but me she forgot,"
declares the Lord.

Historically, people were told that this woman was

interpreted as a marriage between God and Israel. However, if you do a careful reading of Hosea in its totality, it clearly identifies Israel as a child of Yahweh. Therefore it can't be married to Yahweh. Yahweh also continues in this Hosea speech to strip her naked and sets her out into the desert to expose her private parts, to shame her and subjugate her. This is not vulgar behavior you would attribute to a country. This is a very specific way of talking about the treatment of women.

Later, he reconciles with her by luring her into the wilderness and telling her that she can call him "my husband" not "my master." But he adds, "I will remove the names of Baals from her lips; no longer will their names be invoked…. And you will acknowledge the Lord."

Yahweh finalized his divorce from Asherah through words but wasn't able to wipe her out entirely. Feminine manifestations of divinity were methodically and sometimes violently opposed by the religious authorities of the King of Judah and its Temple. Yet as her statues resurfaced, Asherah persisted with the help of feminist theologians and some archaeologists.

In Chinese philosophy, yin and yang—bright/dark, positive/negative—describe how seemingly opposite or contrary forces may actually be complementary, interconnected, and interdependent in the natural world and how they may give rise to each other as they interrelate. Many tangible dualities such as light and dark, fire and water, expanding and contracting are thought of as physical manifestations of the duality symbolized by yin and yang.

Ancient people observed the nature and universe very closely and came up with the yin yang concept. In their eyes, no single being or form could exist unless it was seen in relation to its surrounding environment. By simplifying these relationships, they tried to explain complicated phenomena in the universe.

The yin yang sign is a symbol of harmony and completeness. Yin is the passive, sustaining principle of the universe, characterized as female and associated with earth, dark, and cold. Yang is the active, creative principle of the universe, characterized as male and associated with heaven, heat, and light. Ohsawa writes, "If man continues to become more feminine—losing his Yang qualities—and woman continues to become more masculine—losing her Yin qualities—the end result can be the end of the human race. What we are witnessing at this moment is merely the prelude to that tragedy."

Removing Asherah from the original story, if nothing else, weakened the yin in human nature and sacred relationships and created too much yang. This has emasculated men and masculinized women. Rather than having harmonious unities, couples experience stress and pressure. Rather than enjoy the opposite sex, we somehow learned to be in regular conflict with them. Most love songs today are about pain, suffering, and breakups. Films and TV shows promote divorce as the answer to an unhappy spouse or demean marriage by portraying most as dysfunctional while, on the other side, creating a romantic fantasy about weddings so people keep "falling in love" rather than "rising in love."

The relationship between men and women should resemble the marriage of heaven and earth. The sun and the moon don't fight about their roles or get bored performing their daily routines. They know their purpose in the world and execute it day in and day out in harmony, regardless of weather or catastrophic events. They have a rhythmic dance. To have a similar union, we must honor the higher purpose of coming together and embrace the long-term responsibilities without getting caught up in the illusion of romance and a fairytale wedding.

Chapter 14

Lilith and Eve
The First Women

There are two different Creation accounts of women in the Bible. In Genesis 1, living things appear in a specific order: plants, then animals, then finally man and woman are made simultaneously on the sixth day. "Male and female He created them" (Genesis 1:27). In this version of human origins, man and woman, "humankind," are created together and appear to be equal. In Genesis 2, however, man is created first, followed by plants, then animals and finally woman. She comes last because in the array of wild beasts and birds that God had created, "no fitting helper was found" (Genesis 2:20). The Lord therefore casts a deep sleep upon Adam and returns to work, forming woman from Adam's rib. God presents woman to Adam, who approves of her and names her Eve. One traditional interpretation of this second Creation story, which scholars identify as the older of the two accounts, is that woman is made to please man and is subordinate to him.

Considering every word of the Bible to be accurate and sacred, commentators needed a story to explain the disparity in the Creation narratives of Genesis 1 and 2. God creates woman twice—once with man, once from man's rib—so there must have been two women. They developed in Jewish literature a complex interpretive system called the *midrash*, which attempts to reconcile biblical contradictions and bring new meaning to the scriptural text. Employing both a philological method and often an ingenious imagination, midrashic writings, which reached their height in the second century CE, influenced later Christian interpretations of the Bible. Inconsistencies in the story of Genesis, especially the two separate accounts of creation, received particular attention. Later, beginning in the thirteenth century CE, such questions were also taken up in Jewish mystical literature known as the Kabbalah.

In order to complete the story, the midrashic literature identifies Adam's first wife as Lilith and his second wife as Eve. Only when Lilith rebelled and abandoned Adam did God create Eve, in the second account, as a replacement. It explains that at the time Jehovah created Adam, he created a woman, Lilith, who like Adam was taken from the earth. She was given to Adam as his wife. But there was a dispute between them about a matter that when it came before the judges had to be discussed behind closed doors. She spoke the unspeakable name of Jehovah and vanished.

In the *Alpha Betha of Ben Sira*, an anonymous collection of midrashic proverbs probably compiled in the eleventh century CE, it is explained more explicitly that the conflict arose because Adam, as a way of asserting his authority over Lilith, insisted that she lie beneath him during sex. Lilith, however, considering herself to be Adam's equal, refused to lie beneath him, and after pronouncing the Ineffable Name (i.e. the magic name of God) flew off into the ethers as a winged creature with talons as feet.

Adam, distraught and no doubt also angered by her insolent behavior, wanted her back. On Adam's request, God sent three angels, named Senoy, Sansenoy, and Semangelof, who found her in the Red Sea. Despite the threat from the three angels that if she didn't return to Adam one hundred of her sons would die every day, she refused, claiming that she was created expressly to harm newborn infants. However, she did swear that she would not harm any infant wearing an amulet with the images and/or names of the three angels on it.

At this point, the legend of Lilith as the "first Eve" merges with the earlier legend of Sumero-Babylonian origin, dating from around 3,500 BCE of Lilith as a winged female demon who kills infants and endangers women in childbirth. In this role, she was one of several *mazakim*, or "harmful spirits," known from incantation formulas preserved in Assyrian, Hebrew, and Canaanite inscriptions intended to protect against them. As a female demon, she is closely related to

Lamashtu, whose evilness included killing children, drinking the blood of men, and eating their flesh. Lamashtu also caused pregnant women to miscarry, disturbed sleep, and brought nightmares.

In turn, Lamashtu is like another demonized female called Lamia, a Libyan serpent goddess whose name is probably a Greek variant of Lamashtu. Like Lamashtu, Lamia killed children. In the guise of a beautiful woman, she also seduced young men. In the Latin Vulgate Bible, Lamia is given as the translation of the Hebrew Lilith. In other translations, the name means "screech owl" and "night monster". Christopher Witcombe writes, "It needs to be remembered that these demonic 'women' are essentially personifications of unseen forces invented to account for otherwise inexplicable events and phenomena which occur in the real world. Lilith, Lamashtu, Lamia and other female demons like them are all associated with the death of children and especially with the death of newborn infants."

He adds that it may be easily imagined that they were held accountable for such things as Sudden Infant Death Syndrome (SIDS, also called crib death, or cot death) where an apparently healthy infant dies for no obvious reason. Cot death occurs almost always during sleep at night and is the most common cause of death of infants. Its cause still remains unknown.

By inventing evil spirits like Lilith, Lamashtu, and Lamia, parents were not only able to identify the enemy but also to know what they had to guard against. Amulets with the names of the three angels were intended to protect against the power of Lilith. Lilith also personified licentiousness and lust. In the Christian Middle Ages she, or her female offspring, the *lilim*, became identified with succubae, the female counterparts of incubi, who would copulate with men in their sleep, causing them to have nocturnal emissions, or "wet dreams."

Lilith is represented as a powerfully sexual woman against whom men and babies felt they had few defenses and, except for a few amulets, little protection. Much more so than Eve, Lilith is the personification of female sexuality. Her legend serves to demonstrate how, when unchecked, female sexuality is disruptive and destructive.

David Stern and Mark Jay Mirsky write that "another theory about the creation of this Lilith story is that Ben Sira's tale is in its entirety a deliberately satiric piece that mocks the Bible, the Talmud, and other rabbinic exegeses. Indeed, *The Alphabet*'s language is often coarse and its tone irreverent, exposing the hypocrisies of biblical heroes such as Jeremiah and offering 'serious' discussions of vulgar matters such as masturbation, flatulence, and copulation by animals. In this context, the story of Lilith might have been a parody that never represented true rabbinic thought. It may have served as lewd entertainment for rabbinic students and the public, but it was largely unacknowledged by serious scholars of the time."

When Lilith was cursed, God realized that Adam was all alone again and chose to make him a companion. This time in order to ensure that his companion would be obedient, he took one of Adam's own ribs and created Eve. Again I quote Kramer, who wrote, "Why a rib instead of another organ to fashion the woman whose name Eve means according to the Bible, 'she who makes live'? If we look at the Sumerian myth, we see that when Enki gets ill, cursed by Ninhursag, one of his body parts that start dying is the rib. The Sumerian word for rib is 'ti.' To heal each of Enki's dying body parts, Ninhursag gives birth to eight goddesses. The goddess created for the healing of Enki's rib is called Nin-ti, the lady of the rib. But the Sumerian word 'ti' also means 'to make live.' The name 'Nin-ti' may therefore mean 'the lady who makes live' as well as 'the lady of the rib.' Thus, a very ancient literary pun was carried over and perpetuated in the Bible, but without its original meaning, because the Hebrew word for 'rib' and that for 'who makes live' have nothing in common. Moreover, it is Ninhursag who gives her life essence to heal Enki, who is then reborn from her."

God planted a garden in Eden with every good thing. All was as it should be, ordered and calm. But God also created an independent and strong-minded woman who, like all humans, was both creative and destructive, clever and short-sighted: Eve, the first woman. What does she do?

She explores the Garden, she meets and interrogates the snake, she makes a decision, then returns to Adam and makes suggestions for a course of action. She is expelled from Eden, moving humanity out of the Garden. Death came to the whole human race as a result of what Eve was tricked into doing and Adam's subsequent choice to sin. Two specific curses were given to Eve and all her daughters. First, God multiplied Eve's pain in childbearing. Second, God pronounced that the relationship between man and woman would be characterized by conflict (Genesis 3:16).

These two curses have proven to be true in every woman's life throughout history. No matter how many medical advances we achieve, childbearing is always a painful and stressful experience for a woman. And no matter how advanced and progressive society becomes, the relationship between men and women remains a power struggle, a battle of the sexes, full of strife.

Nowadays, Lilith has become a symbol of freedom for many feminist groups. Due to the rising level of education in numerous cultures, many women understand that they can be independent, so they began looking for symbols of feminine power. Lilith also started to be worshiped by some followers of the pagan Wicca religion, which was created in the 1950s.

This appeal was enhanced by artists, who took her on as a muse. She became a popular motif in art and literature around the Renaissance period, when Michelangelo portrayed her as a half-woman, half-serpent being. He presented her around the Tree of Knowledge and increased the importance of her legend. With time, Lilith became more attractive for the imaginations of male artists like Dante Gabriel Rosetti, who reimagined and presented her as the most beautiful female being of the world. The author of *The Chronicles of Narnia* series, C.S. Lewis, was inspired by the legend about Lilith when he created the *White Witch*. She was beautiful but dangerous and cruel. He mentioned that she was Lilith's daughter and that she was determined to kill Adam and Eve's children.

When women started to receive more rights, they started to disagree with the man-concentrated vision of the world, including the biblical story about the beginning of life on earth. They made sweeping shifts. Lilith today, for instance, is the name of a national literacy program in Israel and the title of a Jewish women's magazine. The ancient Sumerian legendary female demon is a popular topic in feminist literature related to ancient mythology. Researchers still discuss if she was created as a real demon or as an untrue warning of what may happen if women receive more power.

It is through Lilith as well that women are able to come to terms with the darker sides of their innermost selves, with their own unfulfilled desires and the many dark and painful experiences that they have had to face each and every time they have tried to gain equality with men. There can be no good and bad, black and white, or right and wrong, since human life has many unique and varying qualities to it, and it is Lilith, donning the mask of the dark anima, who teaches women how to take those special qualities and then use them exclusively to their own advantage.

Helen Talia writes that women have been marred with the responsibility of the original sin and eventually the death of all mankind that followed. But in ancient civilizations such as the Sumerians (3500–1750 BC) and in Hinduism (2000 BC), where spirituality was more customary, women were regarded in high esteem and hailed as deities, mainly due to their ability to procreate. Yet as man stayed away from spiritually and scrimmaged into organized religions, the divine being engendered a male-image (one Supreme Being), ruler of all, heaven and earth.

The dominance that birthed Judeo-Christian, and later Islam, three domineering religions, all founded in the Middle East, gave way to the very woman, once hailed, to become the ultimate sacrifice—veiling, stoning, female genital mutilation, and honor killing, despite God clearly commanding in the Sixth Commandment for man not to kill. Yet killing continues, not only of the flesh, but of the genuine idealisms and unique characteristics of women, which, in my personal interpretation, Talia says, is no lesser a crime than breaking the Sixth Commandment.

We still live in an age where an Eve-type of woman is more preferable than a Lilith. Female partners who are beautiful, innocent, devoted, and obedient are vastly desired while being distinctive, outspoken, rebellious, and brainy makes others feel threatened. Such women are often associated with evilness, madness, and, like Lilith, are described as demonic. The truth is that they're simply unique and are individual thinkers. There is a lot to learn from them, if they give themselves the opportunity to flourish while maintaining balance rather than get stuck with the labels people place on them.

It does no one any good to blame men for our lives or for women's circumstances. We've evolved a great deal since the births of Eve and Lilith. Today, we have a lot of opportunities, and we can make a big difference in our families and communities. One way women can make a difference is by coming together and making an effort to move forward in the direction that supports and protects them.

Lilith-types are the ones most likely to be oppressed and abused, especially in some Eastern countries where men expect women to be slaves for men. Women who embody Lilith characteristics might feel so misunderstood, might have such difficulty fitting in, that they turn to harmful paths to sedate their pains and confusion. Their desire for attention, for belonging, keeps them in constant motion. They fail to experience stillness.

Stillness fills our void, a void that cannot be filled with material things. Without stillness and sacredness, people can get stuck on addictions to substances like drugs, food, and alcohol as well as behavioral patterns, such as laziness or overwork, and emotions such as sadness, depression, and anger. They endanger themselves to feel alive when they can easily become high on life's mysteries and natural phenomena. This is really what the soul is searching for. When it doesn't find it, it gets jittery, goes through a seizure, in its attempt to find what's missing.

A new report shows that American life expectancy has dropped due to a staggering increase in suicide, which is at a 50-year peak. More than half of the people who died by suicide had no known mental health issues. Their issues had to do with relationships, substance use, health, jobs, or finances.

Stillness will remove distractions and move you to do great things. When a woman embraces stillness, she truly honors who she is as a woman. She becomes centered in peace and wisdom. Women who are not centered are always looking for a new prayer, new clothes, new material objects, new men, because they can't be still. No amount of sex or purses or vacations or pedicures and manicures will keep her happy. Her desires become mumbo jumbo because they are too broad and too many. In her stillness, a woman will learn to focus on one meaningful desire at a time and, in time, she will get what she desires. The universe will respond promptly. But if she has thousands of desires at once, it will take lifetimes to satisfy all of those desires.

Our minds and hearts are like our closets. If we don't get rid of old clothes and shoes or items we no longer use, we will simply mishandle the quality of our space. Soon the crowded clothes and shoes will be less beautiful and attractive, lost in the shuffle. Our attachments to everything, including desires that no longer serve us, keeps us from true inner abundance.

Sit down in silence and ask yourself what is the one thing you want to focus on for the next year? What desires are you willing to give up, because they're holding you back, to help the universe make that one desire happen? Be honest with yourself. If we're honest with ourselves then we can go after the Holy Grail, which symbolizes the vessel that contains miraculous powers and provides us with happiness, eternal youth, and infinite abundance. The ultimate thing is to stand still and hold the world that is moving.

Chapter 15

Kubaba
The only queen on the Sumerian King List

For generations at a time, kingship was bestowed upon a particular city in Mesopotamia, represented by a monarch who ruled for a long time. Only one city was believed to hold true kingship at any given time. After a few hundred years, kingship went from one city to another, which then held the honor of kingship for a few generations. The city that came to importance claimed this divine right, although many cities had individual kings reigning at the same time.

Among the heaps of monarchs whose names are on the Sumerian King List, there's only one woman: Kubaba. She's identified as "the woman tavern keeper." She brewed beer! Since drinking beer was considered a sacred act, women tavern keepers held significant, respectable, and powerful positions in Sumerian mythology and daily life until later periods in Mesopotamia.

Kubaba was a successful businesswoman as a tavern keeper, and she was also successful as a queen. The King List says that she "made firm the foundations of Kish," meaning she protected it against invaders and made it strong. The King List states that she reigned for 100 years from 2500 to 2330 BC. After Kish was defeated, the gods decided to remove kingship from this city and take it to the city of Akshak. Story has it that Kubaba then went back to being the alewife, feeding local fishermen who lived near her house.

The Weidner Chronicle is a propagandistic letter attempting to date the shrine of Marduk at Babylon to an earlier period and alleging to show that each of the kings who had neglected its proper rites had lost the primacy of Sumer. It contains a brief account of the rise of "the house of Kubaba" occurring in the reign of Puzur-Nirah of Akshak:

Mesopotamian Goddesses

[38'] In the reign of Puzur-Nirah, king of Akšak, the freshwater fishermen of Esagila

[39'] were catching fish for the meal of the great lord Marduk;

[40'] the officers of the king took away the fish.

[41'] The fisherman was fishing when 7 (or 8) days had passed...

[42'] in the house of Kubaba, the tavern-keeper ... they brought to Esagila.

[42a'] At that time BROKEN anew for Esagila...

[43'] Kubaba gave bread to the fisherman and gave water, she made him offer the fish to Esagila.

[44'] Marduk, the king, the prince of the Apsû, favored her and said: "Let it be so!"

[45'] He entrusted to Kubaba, the tavern keeper, sovereignty over the whole world.

Kubaba's kindness caused the god Marduk to give her royal dominion of all lands. Eventually, royal power went back to Kish after Akshak and this time, Puzur-Sue, the son of Kubaba, became king. He ruled for twenty-five years. Puzur-Suen's son, Ur-Zubaba, ruled after him.

In later generations, Mesopotamians decided it was unnatural for women to uphold traditional roles for men and provided this omen to make sure no other woman dares to improperly cross that line again: "If an androgyny is born, with both rod and vagina—omen of Kubaba, who ruled the country. The country of the king shall be ruined."

They suddenly saw this as violating the natural order of things. The omen writings specify that a person with the sexual organs of two genders and a queen regnant was viewed as unnatural. People felt that Kubaba improperly crossed a boundary and surpassed gender divisions. In another omen reading, if a patient's lung didn't look so good, it was the sign of Kubaba, "who seized the kingship."

Kubaba was later worshiped as a goddess. Shrines in her honor spread throughout Mesopotamia. Relief carvings show her seated, wearing a cylindrical headdress like the polos and holding probably a tympanum, hand drum, or possibly a mirror in one hand and a poppy capsule, or perhaps pomegranate, in the other. As her cult spread across nations, the country of "the king" was evidently ruined because of her absence.

Once, the wife of one of my cousins talked to me about male students from the Arab world who had come to the Ukraine to study. They didn't quite understand the idea of equality and in some regards were disrespectful toward the opposite genders. The girls explained to them, "Girls can rule the world too."

This behavior, of course, is not reserved to men from the Arab world. In film school here in America, I was the only female student in a class of twenty-plus male students. While a number of them treated me as an equal, many, including one of the instructors, dismissed my presence and my willingness to learn. They underestimated my creativity and even made me feel as if I was taking up unnecessary space.

Girls, like boys, can pursue their dreams and manifest them. They only need to appreciate and believe in themselves enough to do so. We are all artists or writers or inventors in the becoming. We all have a life song. But we are lost and afraid to own our talents and our success. We're trying to birth something, but we sabotage the very thing we want. We find a way to stop it from happening. We blame a person or circumstances for our failures because, from childhood, we've learned how to point fingers but not how to mother our experiences, our dreams and goals, to reach our ultimate fulfillment.

Talia writes that "until one shares in the responsibility of his or her own behavior, and the necessary social revolution takes place, women, society's other very important half, will remain second-class citizens, and their generosity, gentleness, and wisdom, prevalent for the progression of any nation, will never be fully realized."

There's no master but you. Using tools and guidance from those who have walked before us is important but in the end you are your own master. How do you learn to master yourself? By getting out of your head, putting aside your negative feelings, and using your hands and feet to do the work, you can shift from servant to master. In the process of doing what you want, you can reprogram and manage your thoughts and feelings. You transform yourself from the inside. The act of manifesting aligns the physical, mental, emotional, and spiritual aspects of yourself.

That's what happened in the year 2016, during the presidential campaigns between Hillary Clinton and Donald Trump. Trump winning the elections caused a gender upheaval. Thousands of women stopped analyzing their thoughts and feelings, comparing and contrasting, being jealous, and searching for people to mirror them. Bursting with courage, they stepped into leadership roles and became the mirror. Some say that in 2020, the year of clear vision, the spiritual and mental world will unite. Many believe this is a time for women, with a record number of women elected to the House.

What does this mean for the world? No one can dispute that something is not working right now, that violence, imbalance, and instability is robbing us of peace. A world with women leaders means a likelihood of shifting powers gracefully without a drop of bloodshed. It means less of a conquering mentality and more of an inclusive and embracing attitude, more of an investment in universal wellbeing instead of warfare.

The United States spent $6 trillion on wars that have killed 500,000 people since 9/11. Imagine if America had instead invested that money in its own people and those countries, how much better off everyone would have been? More women leaders means a likelihood that justice will be better served because leadership will be a combination of logic and feelings. It means more role models for girls and young ladies who will realize they don't need to "get a man" or "get to the top" using their sexuality. More girls will learn to allow themselves to be reserved and selective when choosing sexual partners and when choosing approaches to an affluent career.

This is not to say that women are better or worse than men. It's important to recognize that society needs both genders working together to make a better world. Women and men offer so many teachings for each other. Men make bold decisions and don't give in easily to tyrants. Women are great in administration and can restore the peace in the midst of chaos.

Women who get caught up in the men vs. women conflict are not in touch with their core, feminine selves. They have old wounds that need to be healed. Rather than use their natural motherly instincts, their minds are oversaturated with thoughts and they will make their lives and the lives of their sons and husbands miserable. They are basically filled with hate.

If we bake a cake or make love with bad thoughts or emotions, it will not be a delicious cake or good love-making. We have to be connected to Spirit, our highest self, as well as our intellect, emotions, and body to have a world that's founded on fairness instead of supremacy.

To not fall into that us vs. them mentality, make a list of the men you love and how they've made an impact in your life. Whether a father, brother, cousin, spouse, son, or teacher, males have helped us become who we are today. How did the men in your life empower you? This exercise helps move us from a state of victimhood and blame to one of compassion and self-love. It also allows us to enjoy the company of our partners. It's a wonderful way to bless us and them.

Chapter 16

Al-Lat, Al-Uzza and Manat
The Three Trinity

Al-Lat, Al-Uzza, and Manat formed the triple trinity. Legend has it that the people of Mecca were devoted to these goddesses, known as "daughters of Allah." The three of them were very popular goddesses in Mecca at the time of Mohammad. The three daughters of Allah had their sanctuaries in the land which later became the cradle of Islam.

Al-Uzza, whose name means "The Mighty One," was the goddess of the Morning Star. She was one of the most venerated Arab deities and had a temple at Petra, where she may have been the patron goddess of that city. Al-Lat, the Mother, whose name simply means "The Goddess" just as Al-Lah simply means "The God" was the goddess of springtime and fertility, the Earth-Goddess who brings prosperity. She had a sanctuary in the town of Taif, east of Mecca, and was known from Arabia to Iran. Her symbol is the crescent moon, sometimes shown with the sun disk resting in its crescent.

Manat's name is derived from the Arabic word maniya, which means "fate, destruction, doom, death" or menata, which means "part, portion, that which is allotted." She's an ancient deity whose cult may precede both Al-Uzza's and Al-Lat's. Her cult was widespread, though she was particularly worshipped as a black stone at Quidaid, near Mecca. She is connected with the great pilgrimage, as her sanctuary was the starting point for several tribes. She is known from Nabatean inscriptions. Tombs were placed under her protection, their inscriptions asking her to curse violators.

It's said that Khadijah, who was the first wife of Prophet Muhammad, kept an idol of Al-Uzza in her house and worshipped it every evening. Born to a family of high status in the Qurayshi ranks, Khadijah's father was an outstanding tribal leader and well-established businessman whose merchant company thrived. She herself was a successful and esteemed businesswoman known as "Al Tahirah," the pure. She became a widow twice and had children from both husbands before she asked Muhammad to marry her. Even though she was fifteen years older than him and with children, he accepted her proposal and became her third husband. Not only that, but she was the only one of his wives whom he remained monogamous with.

For centuries before Muhammad was born, Allah was

the *Al-Ilah*, chief god, among the 360 gods and goddesses engraved on the walls of the Kaaba. Some say that the 360 pagan idols, later destroyed by Muhammad, did not refer to literal statues or engravings but rather to a spiritual concept relating to the soul, the chakras, and the attainment of enlightenment. From a numerological perspective, 360 adds up to the important occult number nine (3+6+0 = 9). Nine is an important number because it ties to the Magnum Opus, or spiritual enlightenment.

Allah was the Mesopotamian moon god who had three daughters and no sons. While the people of Mecca believed that Allah, the moon god, was the greatest of all gods and the supreme deity in a pantheon of deities, Muhammad said that Allah was not only the greatest god but the only god. He longed to convert the people of Mecca to Islam, a word which translates to submission and obedience to God. But he was met with much resistance and hostility.

In the beginning, in an attempt to appease the Meccans, Muhammad recognized these three powerful deities of Makkah and al-Madinah and made a compromise in their favor, thus permitting prayer to them—a violation of monotheism. He recited these verses of Surat an-Najm, considered a revelation by angel Gabriel: "Have you thought of Al-Lat and Al-Uzza, and Manat, the third, the other? These are the exalted *gharaniq*, whose intercession is hoped for." The word *gharaniq* was difficult to discern and was used only once in the text. Analysts wrote that it meant the cranes. By this revelation, Muhammad acknowledged these three female deities as worthy of worship and whose intercession in heaven was to be sought.

When the Quraysh, Muhammad's family as well as Khadija's, heard those favorable words about their gods, they rejoiced. So they accepted Islam. Later, Muhammad retracted the revelation. He said the angel Gabriel came and chastised him for uttering these verses and informed him that Satan, not Allah, had put these words in Muhammad's mouth. Gabriel said, "O Muhammad, what have you done! You have recited to the people something which I have not brought you from God, and you have spoken what He did not say to you." Thus, it was said that Satan had tempted the prophet to utter the line "These are the exalted cranes whose intercession is to be hoped for." This was later referred to as the Satanic Verses.

Gabriel adds (Quran 53:21) "That is, you held these goddesses as daughters of Allah, Lord of the worlds, and did not consider while inventing this absurd creed that as for yourself you regarded the birth of a daughter as disgraceful, and desired to have only male children, but as for Allah you assign to Him only daughters." He rants that angels would not be given the names of females and it's a folly to regard them as females and daughters of Allah.

Shortly after the Conquest of Mecca, Muhammad aimed to eliminate the last idols reminiscent of pre-Islamic practices. He sent Khalid ibn Al-Walid during Ramadan 630 AD to a place called Nakhlah, where the goddess Al-Uzza, considered the most important goddess in the region, was worshipped by the tribes of Quraish and Kinanah. Khalid set out with thirty horsemen to destroy the shrine. It appears that there were two idols of Al-Uzza, one real and one fake. Khalid first located the fake and destroyed it then returned to the prophet to report that he had fulfilled his mission.

"Did you see anything unusual?" asked the prophet.

"No," replied Khalid.

"Then you have not destroyed Al-Uzza," said the prophet.

"Go again."

Angry at the mistake that he had made, Khalid once again rode to Nakhla, and this time he found the real temple of Al-Uzza. The custodian of the temple of Al-Uzza had fled for his life, but before forsaking his goddess he had hung a sword around her neck in the hope that she might be able to defend herself. As Khalid entered the temple, he was faced by an unusual naked dark woman who stood in his way and wailed. Khalid did not stop to decide whether this woman might be there to seduce him or to protect the idol, so he drew his sword in the name of Allah and with one powerful stroke the woman was cut in two. He then smashed the idol, and when he returned to Mecca, gave the prophet an account of what he had seen and done. Then the prophet said, "Yes, that was Al-Uzza; and never again shall she be worshiped in your land."

Initially, Muslims continued to mingle with pagan Arabs in the hajj. Eventually, however, the prophet gave the pagans four months to convert to the new religion or be killed. Then, only Muslims were allowed to approach the Kaaba. The year of his death by poisoning, Muhammad led his followers in the traditional ceremonies used by pre-Islamic Arabs, making it part of Islam. Some elements of Hajj and Umrah are very similar to what Arabians used to do in traditional rituals; for example, they would throw rocks at Satan, circle the Kaaba, and kiss the black stone.

Khadija was a strong, independent, wealthy wife, mother, and businesswoman who knew what she wanted and freely pursued it. She was from a clan whose feminine beliefs empowered her. She excelled in business as well as personal life and had an outstanding reputation along the way, proving that the freedom of women does not destroy a man's masculinity. She lived over 1400 years ago, when women were supposed to have been oppressed and buried alive, and yet women like her today are rare in the Middle East. They exist, but they are not the norm.

Women in pre-Islamic era were permitted to rule their tribe and own real estate as well as be self-employed. Some Arab tribes did participate in infanticide, which Muhammad abolished, but obviously not all of them. However, given the violence of that region, particularly toward women, it would be untrue to say that since then, women have been protected, empowered, and honored publicly. They have not been truly celebrated, heard, or respected. According to the 2017 Global Gender Gap Report, eighteen of the bottom twenty countries are predominately Muslim countries. We can fight and argue about this in our heads as much as we want, but when it comes to facts, the truth contradicts the idealism.

Too many people have the attitude "Give me the silver bullet of truth." But truths change with time. The only constant is change. The *I-have-it-all-figured-out-and-most-people-don't* type of thinking keeps us small. None of us have it all figured out, and those that think they do tend to follow mindlessly and blindly. They tend to see things one way, with an attitude that it's their way or the highway. Of course, they're always on the righteous side, and their government, institution, and religious affiliation is the only path to salvation and freedom. They are usually quite smug about their beliefs whether it's of a political, social, intellectual or spiritual nature. They end up following a politician or guru or heroic academic who will rob them of their soul and savings. They will blame blacks or whites, the rich or the poor, the young or the old for their troubles. They prefer either conventionality or its extreme opposite because its black-and-white solution is easier for them to accept and it gives them a sense of privilege.

Through misguidance and ignorance passed on from one generation to the next, people were taught limitations, superstition, and shame. Rather than encouraged to know themselves, be independent thinkers and responsible individuals, they're told from an early age to seek salvation rather than answers. Rather than question stories full of contradictions and hundreds of thousands of diverse interpretations, they'd prefer to follow the status quo. They fear the answers will dismantle the morals they've built even if critical thinking could prevent future wars and lead to peace, happiness, and enlightenment.

Many thought that World War I would be the war to end all wars. But there have been many wars since then because men keep fighting in God's name with people who claim to love others using God as their reason to murder.

Kriwaczek writes, "As in biblical times, God took to speaking to men again, instructing the makers of history. At a secret meeting between senior army officers in Kuwait during the run-up to the First Gulf War, Saddam had explained that he had invaded Kuwait on heaven's express instructions: 'May God be my witness, that it is the Lord who wanted what happened to happen. This decision we received almost readymade from God… Our role in the decision was almost zero.' In a BBC documentary, broadcast in October 2005, Nabil Sha'ath, Foreign Minister of the Palestinian authority recalled that 'President Bush said to all of us: 'I'm driven with a mission from God. God would tell me, 'George, go and fight those terrorists in Afghanistan.' And I did; and then God would tell me 'George, go and end the tyranny in Iraq...' And I did. And now, again, I feel God's words coming to me.'"

My mother's therapist, an Iranian man of Mesopotamian origins, once told me that in 1979, six months before the revolution in Iran and the overthrow of the Shah, the government tested their influence on people by telling them that if they looked at the full moon that night, they would see Ayatollah Khomeini's face. The next morning, the majority claimed that they did see his face and began to consider him a holy man.

So many people say they are awake while still hardcore sleeping. We started at a young age, as babies, having heavenly experiences, suckling from our mother's breasts. As we get older, we begin to lose one thing at a time—a tooth, money, our nice figure, our youth, innocence, and freedoms, and we become burned out. We become disillusioned and suffer as a consequence, all because we're afraid to discover our inner truth and individual sacred path.

The less we remember our inner power, the more dependent we become on people and institutions who claim to know the right answer, the right path, for us. To remember, all we have to do is listen—listen to our feelings and intuition, listen without judgment to other peoples' perspectives, listen with your emotions and not just your mind as you take in information.

Do your research and don't be attached to your discovery. If you become too attached, you risk losing your innocence, motivation, and passions and you'll experience soul sickness. Soul sickness, or demoralization, is characterized by feelings of hopelessness and helplessness and a perceived sense of incompetence. Conflicts and unnecessary struggles prevent us from experiencing growth and joy. Take the good, abandon the bad, and carry on. Nobody has the absolute truth. Reserve your energy to do beneficial work with your findings. Before embarking on a new project or path, ask yourself, what is this actually about and who is this really helping?

Chapter 17

Other Deities

There were dozens of other names of deities who either assimilated to greater goddesses or have lesser influence over the region of ancient Mesopotamia. One thing is for sure, Mesopotamian goddesses have many stories tied to their names. They are associated with almost everything that is found on earth. Their power and dedication cannot be described in words, although I've attempted to do so in this book as best as I could.

Aruru Although she has an important role in Mesopotamian mythology (she was the creator of humankind), Aruru has a small role in the *Epic of Gilgamesh*. But it's a very important one. When the people of Uruk beg Anu for some relief from King Gilgamesh at the beginning of the epic, he delegates the task to Aruru, who creates a new man from clay—Enkidu.

She also shows up during the Flood story in Tablet 1, where she is referred to by an alternate name: Beletili. According to Utnapishtim, who tells the Flood story, Aruru/Beletili is one of the deities who crowd around the sacrifice made by Utnapishtim and his wife after they get out of the ship. Aruru makes her presence felt by suggesting that they ban the god Enlil from the sacrifice since Enlil was the one responsible for the Flood. Even though she isn't successful, one can see where Aruru is coming from: given that humankind is her creation, she can't be expected to take kindly to the guy who tried to wipe it out.

Ashnan was the goddess of grain in Mesopotamia. She and her brother Lahar, both children of Enlil, were created by the gods to provide the Anunnaki with food, but when the heavenly creatures were found unable to make use of their products, humankind was created to provide an outlet for their services.

Aya is Akkadian for "dawn" and by the Akkadian period she was firmly associated with the rising sun and with sexual love and youth. The Babylonians sometimes referred to her as kallatu (the bride), and as such she was known as the wife of Shamash. In fact, she was worshiped as part of a separate-but-attached cult in Shamash's e-babbar temples in Larsa and Sippar.

By the Neo-Babylonian period at the latest, and possibly much earlier, Shamash and Aya were associated with a practice known as Hasadu, which is loosely translated as a "sacred marriage." A room would be set aside with a bed, and on certain occasions the temple statues of Shamash and Aya would be brought together and laid on the bed to ceremonially renew their vows.

Kishar is the daughter of the first children of Apsu and Tiamat. She is the child of Lahamu and Lahmu, the wife, sister and principle of Anshar who is the male principle. Furthermore, she is Anu's mother too. Represented as the counterpart of the sky, Anshar, she is the goddess of mother earth. Her name also states the meaning "Whole Earth." She appears in the opening lines of *Enuma Elish* and suddenly disappears later. She is often seen in texts of first millennium BC, where she is equated with Goddess Antu.

Puabi, a Semitic Akkadian who's also called Shabad, was an important Sumerian queen during the First Dynasty of Ur (c.2006 BC). She could have been a high priestess or wife of a king, but strangely there's no mention of her husband. She died in her forties, assuming she'd outlived her sons and husband, her father and brother Gilgamesh.

Puabi means "Word of the Father." Her tomb, adjoining that of her spouse, was discovered at the Royal Cemetery of Ur, the city famed in the Bible as the home of biblical patriarch Abraham, discovered at the excavations during the 1920s and 1930s by British archaeologist Leonard Woolley. Woolley uncovered some 1,800 burials. He classified sixteen as royal based on their distinctive form, their wealth, and that they included the burials of household servants, male and female, along with high-ranking personages.

A five-foot woman, she was buried with fifty-two attendants: servants, guards, horses, lions, a chariot, and several other bodies. They're suspected of poisoning themselves, or being poisoned by others, to serve their mistress in the next world. Her tomb had been untouched by looters through the millennia with well-preserved grave goods that included a magnificent, heavy gold headdress made of twenty golden leaves, rings, plates, and flowers. Used as a "head wallet," women could detach leaflets of gold from their headdresses or pendants to purchase things they fancied as they shopped. The royal tombs at Ur also show that women held cylinder seals which indicated an agreement to fulfill the detailed transaction of a contract for services, goods, or other arrangements.

In her grave, there were more exquisite jewelry from Grandma Inanna and Grandma Gula. Her hands held a golden cup. Other objects from Puabi's dressing table were cosmetics, such as a box containing kohl, a black pigment used to highlight the eyes. The cylinder seal bears the name "Abarage," whose identity is unknown, but archaeologist Woolley believed Abarage to be Puabi's husband.

Shala was an ancient Sumerian goddess of grain and the emotion of compassion. The symbols of grain and compassion combine to reflect the importance of agriculture in the mythology of Sumer and the belief that an abundant harvest was an act of compassion from the deities. Traditions identify Shala as wife of the fertility god Dagon, or consort of the storm god Hadad, also called Ishkur.

In ancient depictions, she carries a double-headed mace or scimitar embellished with lion heads. Sometimes she is depicted as being borne atop one or two lionesses. From very early times, she was associated with the constellation Virgo and vestiges of symbolism associated with her have persisted in representations of the constellation to current times, such as the ear of grain, even as the deity name changed from culture to culture.

Shamhat, which means the luscious one, is a female character who appears in Tablets I and II of the *Epic of Gilgamesh*. She's also mentioned in Tablet VII. She is a sacred lover and plays a significant role in bringing the wild man Enkidu into contact with civilization. She tames Enkidu, created by the gods as the rival to the mighty Gilgamesh. This causes his former companions, the wild animals, to turn away from him in fright at the watering hole where they congregated. Shamhat persuades him to follow her and join the civilized world in the city of Uruk, where Gilgamesh is king, rejecting his former life in the wild with the animals of the hills.

Gilgamesh and Enkidu become best of friends and undergo many adventures together. When Enkidu is dying he expresses his anger at Shamhat for making him civilized, blaming her for bringing him to the new world of experiences that led to his death. He curses her to become an outcast. The god Shamash reminds Enkidu that Shamhat fed and clothed him. Enkidu relents and blesses her, saying that all men will desire her and offer her gifts of jewels.

Siduri - In the earlier Old Babylonian version of the Epic, Siduri attempts to dissuade Gilgamesh in his quest for immortality, urging him to be content with the simple pleasures of life. In the later Akkadian, also referred to as the standard version of the Epic, Siduri's role is somewhat less important. The above quotation is omitted, and it is instead attributed to the flood hero Utnapishtim, the Mesopotamian precursor to Noah, who discusses issues about life and death. Siduri, nonetheless, has a long conversation with Gilgamesh, who boasts of his exploits and is forced to explain why his appearance is so haggard. When he asks for help in finding Utnapishtim, Siduri explains the difficulties of the journey but directs him to Urshanabi, the ferryman, who may be able to help him cross the subterranean ocean and the ominous "waters of death."

Tashmetum is an Akkadian goddess whose name means "She Who Grants Requests." She is the consort of the god Nabu and they both shared a temple in the city of Borsippa, where they were patron deities. She is virtuous, a loyal wife, and is called upon to listen to prayers and to grant requests.

Chapter 18

Mother of God

I started this project as an act of love for my ancestors and to honor the female deities that had been forgotten for thousands of years. Despite its rich history, for the most part, up until the 2003 US-led invasion, people knew little about Iraq. They didn't realize Iraq was associated with Mesopotamia and they were not aware of the contributions Mesopotamia made to our modern-day civilization. This was partly due to its name change from Mesopotamia to Iraq, which happened after World War I, when in 1921 the British created the Kingdom of Iraq.

I grew up not knowing much about my Chaldean heritage. In Baghdad, where I was born, schools didn't teach history that occurred before Islam some 1400 years ago. There were, however, selective history courses at universities that taught about ancient Mesopotamia. Chaldeans and Assyrians, cultures that endured persecution under the Ottoman Empire and oppression in a war-torn land ruled by dictators, did not have the freedom or resources to keep their culture and heritage alive. They were, for instance, discouraged from speaking their mother tongue, Sureth, in public, which is a form of Aramaic.

This wasn't the case in certain towns in northern Iraq, in the province of Mosul, areas which were almost exclusively inhabited by Christians. Yet even that situation in northern Iraq dramatically changed in 2014 when the Islamic State invaded their villages and forced them out of the region. The attacks caused the Chaldeans, Assyrians, Syriacs, and other minority groups such as the Yazidis in the United States to place greater efforts into assisting their relatives abroad. The attacks also inspired these communities to work harder to preserve their stories, heritage, and language.

During my research while working on this book, I discovered truths I was completely unaware of. Unlike what we've been made to believe, women in ancient Mesopotamia did have rights and female deities were not evil. They wrote poetry about love, longing, home, suffering, hopes, and dreams. They performed miracles. Inanna resurrected her consort—similar to what the prophet Elijah did and the prophet after him, Elisha.

They had plenty of feelings and plenty of stories.

Today we still participate in many cultural customs that originated in ancient Mesopotamia, including using calendars, wearing wedding rings and crosses, singing hymns and carols, and celebrating Christmas, Easter, and St. Valentine's Day. Even the names of our days are associated with that region. There, astrologers assigned each day of the week the name of a god. Many centuries later, the Romans adopted the names to fit their own gods when they began to use the seven-day week.

Thus, Sunday is Sun's day. Monday comes from the Anglo-Saxon monandaeg, which is the Moon's day. On this day, the people gave homage to the goddess of the moon. Tuesday is the first to be named after a Germanic god—Tiu, or Twia—associated with Mars, and so on. Some religious institutions have created a long list of words that are considered pagan-rooted and therefore offensive to Yahweh and say it should be replaced. The proper word for God would be the Mighty One, or Elohim; Church ought to be replaced with Qahal, which means "Assembly of Called Out Ones." Angel should be replaced with messenger and holy with set-apart or dedicated to God.

Neale Donald Walsch writes, "In an earliest part of your history, you lived on this planet in a matriarchal society. Then there was a shift, and the patriarchy emerged. When you made that shift, you moved away from expressing your emotions. You labeled it 'weak' to do so. It was during this period that males also invented the devil and the masculine God."

Stories have power. They can create the reality we live in. One need only take a glimpse at the Middle East to realize the harm that dismissing the divine feminine from God's equation, from God's story, has caused. It is no wonder that region is full of violence and aggression. For thousands of years they tried to live without honoring their counterpart, women. The thirst to wipe away the feminine energy, "her story," in the Middle East succeeded, causing that region to become so imbalanced that no amount of international or supernatural intervention seems able to heal it.

During the last hundred years, the desert sand began to release its hold on the secrets of this captivating civilization, and people continue to learn more about it. Recently, a massive four-thousand-years-old structure was discovered in the Mesopotamian City of Ur. Its walls are nine feet thick, with rows of rooms encircling a large courtyard. Perhaps the twentieth century was meant to be the time for the Sumerian tablets to return to the world, to serve their purpose, to warn future generations about their society's futures and preserve the truth.

By returning to the world, the tablets made a difference. Over the years, Hebrew and Christian writings began to portray the feminine side of God and to include Her into the equation. Since the 1980s, some new translations of the Bible changed the words He or Man to "human beings." One community for Christian Exploration calls God "your Parent" instead of "your Father." The Holy Spirit is a she, Jesus is a he, and the translation words avoid using a pronoun for God.

The Methodist Church introduced a new service book in 1999 which uses both male and female language for God, "Our Father and Our Mother." In 1996, Gates of Repentance, the High Holy Day prayer book of Reform Judaism, was published, calling God "sovereign" instead of "king," and "source" or "parent" instead of "father." Christianity and Judaism are in the process of continuous modification. All language describing God is symbolic and limited by our human understanding. Using feminine, masculine, and non-gendered images for God is a good thing because women are not second-class citizens in the Kingdom of God. Her nature is drawn directly from the nature of God.

While there has been no similar undertaking in Islam, there are a handful of female-led mosques in the west, from Copenhagen to Los Angeles, with women who are trying to change a narrative that has been patriarchal for centuries by having their own mosque and leading it. They want to rewrite a male-dominated way of worship.

Dr. Bettany Hughes writes, "Whenever I feel sad about how systematically women vanished from history, I take the long view, and say, there has been a problem here for at least 3,500 years, so it's no surprise that we have some catching up to do! But that in itself is quite empowering, because we know what we are up against. This is an issue that has very deep roots, and we can see how and why that plays out, and therefore what we can do to start to change things."

We have the power to shape society through words, symbols, prayers and images of God, to make society more just and good. In a world that so often and in so many ways degrades and disrupts the humanity of women, our theology and admiration of God can help us celebrate women. It can help reshape our conditions. Storytellers make use of the past to give vivid depictions of what Earth may be like hundreds of years from now.

Imagine what the world would be like if all the money and expertise that is now being spent to create weapons were channeled into areas that can benefit people rather than kill them? Think about a world in which people are in balance with their physical, emotional, spiritual, and intellectual selves and, as a result, heart disease, cancer, malaria, or other ailments including mental illness, is not widespread. Foresee a world where self-care is the norm and there is no need for hospitals and medications. Picture an earth which produces enough food and natural remedies for everyone with all having access to it. Develop the vision of a Dilmun, a paradise on earth, as you gather personal power and strengthen your relationship with the Creator. A Dilmun is already within you and will remain there as long as you remember and nurture your dreams, live your truth, follow your destiny, trust yourself, and find your way home.

Notes

The literary works of Mesopotamia, written in cuneiform around 3200 B.C., were utterly unknown until the mid-nineteenth century CE when men like George Smith and Henry Rawlinson (1810-1895 CE) interpreted the language and translated it into English. Many biblical texts were thought to be original works until cuneiform was decoded.

In *Mesopotamian Goddesses: Unveiling Your Feminine Power*, several descriptions of these ancient texts were used from various sources to write each goddess' story.

Chapter 1

George Smith, *The Chaldean Account of Genesis* (New York: Scribner, Armstrong & Co. 1876), p. 22. Smith was an English Assyriologist who first discovered and translated the *Epic of Gilgamesh* and the Mesopotamian version of the Flood Story, which until then was thought to be original to the biblical Book of Genesis.

Ur of the Chaldeas—Geoff Simons, *Iraq: From Sumer to Saddam* (New York: St. Martin's Press, Scholarly and Reference Division, 1994), p.119-120.

Charles Chipiez and Georges Perrot - *A History of Art in Chaldea & Assyria, v. 1 & 2* (New York: A. C. Armstrong and Son, 1884).

Genesis chapter 10, commonly known as the Table of Nations, is a list of the patriarchal founders of seventy nations which descended from Noah through his three sons, Shem, Ham, and Japheth. It's about their dispersion into many lands after the Flood.

The name Chaldean—William D. Barrick, Th.D. "Ur of the Chadeans (GEN 11:28-31): A Model for Dealing with Difficult Texts," quoting Gleason L. Archer, Jr., "Modern Rationalism and the Book of Daniel," *Bibliotheca Sacra* 136/542 (April 1979): p. 137.

The inhabitants of Chaldea - George Roux, *Ancient Iraq* (New York: Penguin Random House, 1993), p. 281.

Semites - *World Book Encyclopedia* (Chicago: W.F. Quarrie & Company, 1929).

One supreme deity - *World Book Encyclopedia*. (Chicago, IL: W.F. Quarrie & Company, 1929).

Nabopolassar—Henry W.F. Saggs, "Nebuchadrezzar II: King of Babylonia," *Encyclopedia Britannica,* accessed June 1, 2018, www.britannica.com/biography/Nebuchadrezzar-II#ref98254.

Hanging Gardens—Geoff Simons, *Iraq: From Sumer to Saddam* (New York: St. Martin's Press, Scholarly and Reference Division, 1994), p. 129.

Astronomy and astrology relating to Chaldeans—Becca, Joey, Lena, and Lexi "Astrology and Astronomy," *Chaldeans*, accessed August 17, 2018, http://chaldeansapter.weebly.com/accomplishments.html.

Helena Petrovna Blavatsky, *Isis Unveiled: A Master-Key to the Mysteries of Ancient and Modern Science and Theology Vol. I & II* (J.W. Bouton Booksellers, New York: 1877), p. 62.

In Early Bronze Age Mesopotamia –Sierra Helm [quoting Anne Baring and Jules Cashford's book *The Myth of the Goddess: Evolution* *of an Image* (London: Arkana, 1993, p. 184)] "The Passion for the Goddess; a Comparative Study on the Reverence of the Goddess in Contemporary America and Ancient Mesopotamia" (PhD diss., Roger Williams University, May 3, 2011).

Bettany Hughes, "Why Were Women Written Out of History?" *English Heritage*, February 29, 2016, http://blog.english-heritage.org.uk/women-written-history-interview-bettany-hughes.

Merlin Stone, *When God Was a Woman* (Wilmington, NC: Mariner Books, 1978), p. 105.

Nuah, the universal Mother—Helena Petrovna Blavatsky, *The Theosophical Glossary* (London: The Theosophical Publishing Society, 1892), p. 796.

Patricia Monaghan, PhD. *Encyclopedia of Goddesses and Heroines* (Novato, California: New World Library, 2014 - Originally published in 1981), p. 29.

Leonard Shlain, *The Alphabet versus the Goddess: The Conflict Between Word and Image* (New York: Penguin Books, 1999), p. 6-7.

Chapter 2

The Enûma Eliš is the Babylonian creation myth. It was recovered by Austen Henry Layard in 1849 in the ruined Library of Ashurbanipal at Nineveh. A form of the myth was first published by George Smith in 1876 in his book *The Chaldean Account of Genesis*. Active research and further excavations led to near completion of the texts and improved translation.

Chaoskampf—Stephanie Dalley, *Myths from Mesopotamia* (Oxford, UK:

Oxford University Press, 1987), p. 329.

Robert Graves, *The Greek Myths* (New York: Penguin, 1960).

Edward Chiera, *They Wrote on Clay: The Babylonian Tablets Speak Today* (Chicago, IL: The University of Chicago Press, 1938), p. 125.

Jean Shinoda Bolen, M.D. *Goddesses in Every Woman: A New Psychology of Women* (New York: Harper Collins, 1984).

Joseph Campbell, *A Joseph Campbell Companion: Reflections on the Art of Living* (San Anselmo, California: Joseph Campbell Foundation, 2011), p. 117.

Mary Beard, *Women & Power: A Manifesto* (New York: Liveright, 2017).

Chapter 3

Black, J.A., Cunningham, G., Fluckiger-Hawker, E, Robson, E., and Zólyomi, G., "Enki and Ninhursag," *The Electronic Text Corpus of Sumerian Literature*, University of Oxford, updated on December 19, 2006, http://etcsl.orinst.ox.ac.uk/cgi-bin/etcsl.cgi?text=t.1.1.1&charenc=j#.

Samuel Noah Kramer, *History Begins at Sumer* (Philadelphia, Pennsylvania: University of Pennsylvania Press, 1988), p. 143-144.

Zecharia Sitchin, *The Twelfth Planet* (New York: Stein and Day, 1976).

Mark, Joshua J., "Ninhursag," *Ancient History Encyclopedia*, January 26, 2017. www.ancient.eu/Ninhursag.

Daniel Workman, "United States Top 10 Imports," *World Exports*,

September 2, 2018, http://www.worldstopexports.com.

Chapter 4

Dr. Uri Gabbay, "The Sumerian City Laments and the Book of Lamentations: A Comparative Theological View," *The Torah*, July 22, 2015, thetorah.com/the-genre-of-lamentations.

The translations of Sumerian laments in Dr. Uri Gabbay's essay are taken from Mark E. Cohen, *The Canonical Lamentations of Ancient Mesopotamia* (Potomac, MD: Capital Decisions Ltd, 1988) and Nili Samet, *The Lamentation over the Destruction of Ur* (Winona Lake, IN: Eisenbrauns, 2014).

Lament for Ur –International World History Project: World History From the Pre-Sumerian Period to the Present, accessed July 2, 2018, http://history-world.org/lament_for_ur.htm.

Brian Levack, *The Witch-hunt in Early Modern Europe* (New York: Longman, 1995), p. 21-26.

Heinrich Kramer, *Malleus Maleficarum* (originally published in Germany, 1487).

Under the guidance of the *Malleus Maleficarum* - Chloe Berge, "Why Are Women Turning to Witchcraft in 2018?" *Fashion Magazine*, August 29, 2018, fashionmagazine.com/culture/witchcraft-2018.

Ruth Mace, "Why are women accused of witchcraft? Study in rural China gives clue," *The Conversation*, January 8, 2018, theconversation.com/why-are-women-accused-of-witchcraft-study-in-rural-china-gives-clue-89730.

Louise Jackson, "Witches, wives, and mothers: Witchcraft persecution and women's confessions in seventeenth-century England," *Women's History Review* Volume 4—1, 1995, p. 63-84.

Gaia Cloutier, "From Holy to Hunted: The Early Modern Witch Trials as a Catholic Response to Female Mysticism." (PhD diss., Trinity College, Spring 2016), p. 5.

Chapter 5

The Huluppu Tree—Diane Wolkstein and Samuel Noah Kramer, *Inanna, Queen of Heaven and Earth: Her Stories and Hymns from Sumer* (New York: Harper Perennial, 1983), p. 4.

Divorce rate—American Psychological Association, accessed October 10, 2018, www.apa.org/topics/divorce.

Jaggi Vasudev, known as Sadhguru, "Sadhguru on Marriage—Choose Consciously" published March 1, 2015 at Sadhguru YouTube Channel, video, 4:31, www.youtube.com/watch?v=UT_nWVLi4Ws&t=159s.

Dr. Joseph Murphy, *The Power of Your Subconscious Mind* (New York: Bantam Book, 1963), p. 121-122.

Samuel Noah Kramer, *The Sacred Marriage Rite: Aspects of faith, myth, and ritual in ancient Sumer* (Bloomington, IN: Indiana University Press, 1969), p. 49.

Nicola Heath, "The historic tradition of wedding night-virginity testing," *SBS*, January 16, 2018, www.sbs.com.au.

Susan Kent, *Sex and Suffrage in Britain 1860-1914* (New York: Routledge, 1990).

Anderson, C.A., Berkowitz, L., Donnerstein, E., Huesmann, L.R., Johnson, J., Linz, D., Malamuth, N., & Wartella, E., "The Influence of Media Violence on Youth," Sage Journals, December 1, 2003. journals.sagepub.com/doi/10.1111/j.1529-1006.2003.pspi_1433.x.

Gabrielle Blair's tweet which began: "I'm a mother of six, and a Mormon. I have a good understanding of arguments surrounding abortion, religious and otherwise" (@designmom, September 13, 2018).

Black, J.A., Cunningham, G., Fluckiger-Hawker, E, Robson, E., and Zólyomi, G., "Inana's descent to the nether world," *The Electronic Text Corpus of Sumerian Literature*, University of Oxford, updated on December 19, 2006, http://etcsl.orinst.ox.ac.uk/cgi-bin/etcsl.cgi?text=t.1.4.1#.

W. E. Vine, *Vine's Complete Expository Dictionary of Old and New Testament Words* (Nashville, TN: Thomas Nelson, 1996), p. 192.

Sue Ellen Thompson, *Holiday Symbols and Customs* (Aston, PA: Omnigraphs, 1998).

Helen Talia, "The Birth of Inanna," Facebook, March 31, 2010, www.facebook.com/photo.php?fbid=1352702492384&set=a.1622985569292&type=3&theater.

Chapter 6

History of sexually active women - Merlin Stone, *When God Was a Woman* (Wilmington, NC: Mariner Books, 1978), p. 44.

Jaggi Vasudev, known as Sadhguru, "Violence Against

Women—Sadhguru Speaks" published July 23, 2017 at Sadhguru YouTube Channel, video, 25:52, www.youtube.com/watch?v=IHJHVuQ5E5E

George Ohsawa, *You Are All Sanpaku* (New York: Citadel Press Book, 1991), p. 125.

Chapter 7

Black, J.A., Cunningham, G., Fluckiger-Hawker, E, Robson, E., and Zólyomi, G., "Enlil and Sud," *The Electronic Text Corpus of Sumerian Literature*, Oxford, accessed February 18, 2018, http://etcsl.orinst.ox.ac.uk/section1/tr122.htm.

Dale Launderville, *Celibacy in the Ancient World: Its Ideal and Practice in Pre-Hellenistic Israel, Mesopotamia, and Greece* (Collegeville, MN: Liturgical Press, 2010), p. 28-30.

"Enlil and Sud" *Wold History*, June 27, 2015, www.worldhistory.biz/ancient-history/63533-enlil-and-sud.html.

"Enlil: Lord Air/Wind, Master of the Divine Word, Inspirer and Empowerer," *Gateways to Babylon*, accessed February 12, 2018, http://www.gatewaystobabylon.com/gods/lords/lordenlil.html.

Chapter 8

Michelle Hart, "High Priestess Enheduanna: First Named Author in History—5 part documentary," published December 8, 2012 at Michelle Hart YouTube channel, video,
Part 1 (7:45) www.youtube.com/watch?v=fKWPREkvNgk
Part 2 (2:50) www.youtube.com/watch?v=47MWzcWIrgc

Part 3 (13:47) www.youtube.com/watch?v=MFlxslZEAbQ
Part 4 (13:14) www.youtube.com/watch?v=TN9HymgOTNE
Part 5 (4:24) www.youtube.com/watch?v=4NVCiin_O10

Marten Stol, *Women in the Ancient Near East* (Berlin, Germany: De Gruyter Inc. 2016).

Benjamin R. Foster, *The age of Agade: Inventing Empire in Ancient Mesopotamia* (New York: Routledge, December 2015).

"Mesopotamian Priests and Priestesses," History on the Net, accessed Mary 20, 2018, www.historyonthenet.com/mesopotamian-priests-and-priestesses.

Joshua J. Mark, "Enheduanna," *Ancient History Encyclopedia*, March 24, 2014, www.ancient.eu/Enheduanna/

Black, J.A., Cunningham, G., Fluckiger-Hawker, E, Robson, E., and Zólyomi, G., "The Exaltation of Inana (Inana B)," *The Electronic Text Corpus of Sumerian Literature*, accessed April 20, 2018, http://etcsl.orinst.ox.ac.uk/section4/tr4072.htm.

Paul Kriwaczek, *Babylon: Mesopotamia and the Birth of Civilization* (St. Martin's Griffin, 2012).

Tim Staples, "What's the Deal with Female Priests?" Published June 3, 2016 at Catholic Answers YouTube Channel, video, 8:06, www.youtube.com/watch?v=mTPdyz5kcRQ.

Max Shadu, "Priestesses, Power, and Politics," *Suppressed Histories*, accessed September 20, 2018, www.suppressedhistories.net/articles/priestesses.html.

"Questions and Answers about Women's Ordination," *Future*

Church, accessed August 12, 2018, www.futurechurch.org/questions-and-answers-about-womens-ordination.

Adelle M. Banks, "Clergywomen numbers increased significantly in two decades, sometimes equaling men," Religion News, October 10, 2018, religionnews.com/2018/10/18/clergywomen-numbers-increased-significantly-in-two-decades-sometimes-equaling-men.

Chapter 9

Miguel Civil, "A hymn to the beer goddess and a drinking song." In *Studies presented to A. Leo Oppenheim* (Chicago: Oriental Institute, 1964), p. 67-89.

April Holloway, "Alcohol as Medicine Through the Ages," Ancient Origins, January 19, 2014, www.ancient-origins.net/human-origins-science/alcohol-medicine-through-ages-001238.

Hayley Dixon, "The beer belly is a myth, study claims" The Telegraph, February 12, 2013, www.telegraph.co.uk/news/health/news/9864412/The-beer-belly-is-a-myth-study-claims.html.

Amy Roeder, "Advertising's toxic effect on eating and body image," The Harvard T.H. Chan School of Public Health, March 18, 2015, www.hsph.harvard.edu/news/features/advertisings-toxic-effect-on-eating-and-body-image.

Laurie J. Shrage, Robert Scott Stewart, Philosophizing About Sex (Louisville, KY: Broadway Press, 2015) p. 187.

Adee Braun, "Misunderstanding Orange Juice as a Health Drink," The Atlantic, February 6, 2014, www.theatlantic.com/health/archive/2014/02/misunderstanding-orange-juice-as-a-health-drink/283579.

David Gillespie, *How the Diet Industry is Making You Sick, Fat & Poor* (Penguin Random House Australia, January 2016).

Chapter 10

Mark, Joshua J. "Gula," *Ancient History Encyclopedia*, last modified January 18, 2017, www.ancient.eu/Gula/.

Asu and Asipu—Emily K. Teall, "Medicine and Doctoring in Ancient Mesopotamia," *Grand Valley Journal of History*, Vol.3-1, October 2014.

Tzvi Abusch and Karel Toorn, *Mesopotamian Magic: Textual, Historical, and Interpretative Perspectives* (the Netherlands, Brill, 2000).

Johanna Stuckey, "'Going to the Dogs': Healing Goddesses of Mesopotamia" *MatriFocus, Cross Quarterly for the Goddess Woman*, Vol. 5-2, 2006.

Chapter 11

Black, J.A., Cunningham, G., Fluckiger-Hawker, E, Robson, E., and Zólyomi, G., "A hymn to Nanshe," *The Electronic Text Corpus of Sumerian Literature*, University of Oxford, updated on December 19, 2006, http://etcsl.orinst.ox.ac.uk/section4/tr4141.htm.

Barbara G. Walker, *The Woman's Encyclopedia of Myths and Secrets* (New York: HarperCollins, 1983).

Tulika Bahadur, "Gudea's Dream," *On Art and Aesthetics*, as mentioned in H.W. F. Saggs, *The Greatness that was Babylon* (New York: New American Library, 1962). onartandaesthetics.com/2016/01/07/gudeas-dreams.

Samuel Noah Kramer, *The Sumerians: Their History, Culture, and Character* (University of Chicago Press, 1964).

Chapter 12

The story of Greek historian Diodorus Siculus, based on passages from the Loeb Classical Library Edition, 1933 CE, translated by C.H. Oldfather.

The Armenian account of Semiramis—Movses Khorenatsi , *The History of Armenia* written in the fifth century.

Chapter 13

William G. Denver, *Did God Have a Wife?: Archaeology and Folk Religion in Ancient Israel* (Grand Rapids, MI: Eardmans, July 23, 2008).

Darlene Kosnik, *History's Vanquished Goddess ASHERAH: God's Wife: the Goddess Asherah, Wife of Yahweh. Archaeological & Historical Aspects of Syro-Palestinian ... Traditions, Macrocosmically Examined* (Emergent Press, llc., February 21, 2014).

The Epic of Baal—translated from *Ethnic Origin, Language and Literature of the Phoenicians*, phoenicia.org/ethnlang.html.

William Smith, *Smith's Dictionary of the Bible* (Philadelphia, PA: A. J. Holman Company, 1868), p. 302.

George Ohsawa, *You Are All Sanpaku* (New York: Citadel Press Book, 1991).

Chapter 14

Explanation of second woman, a Lilith, in the Bible - An important thirteenth century Kabbalah called the *Sefer ha-Zohar*, The Book of Splendor, written by the Spaniard Moses de Leon (c. 1240-1305).

Christopher Witcombe, "Eve and the Identity of Women," *Witcombe* http://witcombe.sbc.edu/eve-women/1evewomen.html.

David Stern and Mark Jay Mirsky, eds. *Rabbinic Fantasies: Imaginative Narratives from Classical Hebrew Literature* (Yale Judaica Series, 1998).

Two Specific Curses Given to Eve—"Who was Eve in the Bible?" *Got Questions*, attained July 18, 2018, www.gotquestions.org/Eve-in-the-Bible.html.

Mask of dark enigma—"Lilith, Demon-Goddess of Eden," *A Journal of a Poet—the Goddess as My Muse,* http://www.angelfire.com/journal/ofapoet/lilith.html.

Helen Talia, "Gender & Engenderment," *Chicago Tribune*, July 9, 2013, www.chicagotribune.com/suburbs/evanston/community/chi-ugc-article-gender-and-engenderment-2013-07-09-story.html.

"Drug and suicide deaths rise as US life expectancy drops," *BBC News Report*, November 29, 2018, www.bbc.com/news/world-us-canada-46389147.

Neta C. Crawford, "$5.9 Trillion Spent and Obligated on Post-9/11 Wars," *Watson Institute for International and Public Affairs*, November

16, 2018, watson.brown.edu/research/2018/59-trillion-spent-and-obligated-post-911-wars.

Chapter 15

Shrines in Kubaba's honor—The Weidner "Chronicle" mentioning Kubaba from Grayson, A.K., 1975, "Assyrian and Babylonian Chronicles."

Carly Silver, "Kubaba, a Queen Among Kings: Bow Down to this Tavern-Keeper," *Thought Co.*, December 15, 2017, www.thoughtco.com/kubaba-a-queen-among-kings-121164.

Samuel Noah Kramer, *The Sumerians: their history, culture and character* (Chicago, IL: University of Chicago Press: 1964).

Chapter 16

Hisham ibn Al-Kalbi, *The Book of Idols*, translated from the Arabic of *The Kitab Al-Asnam* (Princeton, NY: Princeton University Press, 1952).

Donna Randsalu, "Who Were the Daughters of Allah?" (PhD diss., University of British Columbia, September 1988).

Philip K. Hitti, *History of the Arabs*, (Red Globe Press, 2002 - originally published in 1937).

Brother Andrew, "'Daughter-gate': Allah's Daughters: el-Lat, el-Uzza, and Manat," *The Interactive Bible,* http://www.bible.ca/islam/islam-allahs-daughters.htm.

Paul Kriwaczek, *Babylon: Mesopotamia and the Birth of Civilization* (New York: St. Martin's Griffin, 2012), p. 1-2.

Chapter 17

Ashnan—Samuel Noah Kramer, *The Sumerians: Their History, Culture, and Character* (Chicago, IL: University of Chicago Press, 1964) p. 220 –.

Aya—Karel van der Toorn; Bob Becking; Pieter W. van der Horst, *Dictionary of Deities and Demons in the Bible* (Grand Rapids, MI: Eerdmans, 1999), p. 125-126.

Jeremy Black; Anthony Green, *Gods, Demons and Symbols of Ancient Mesopotamia* (London: British Museum Press, 1998).

Michael Jordan, *Encyclopedia of Gods* (London: Kyle Cathie Limited, 1999).

Kishar—Nicole Brisch, "Ansar and Kisar (god and goddess)," *Ancient Mesopotamian Gods and Goddesses,* Oracc and the UK Higher Education Academy, retrieved August 10, 2018, http://oracc.museum.upenn.edu/amgg/listofdeities/anarandkiar/index.html.

Puabi –
Sir Leonard Woolley, *Ur Excavations II, The Royal Cemetery* (London-Philadelphia, 1934).

M. Vidale, "Royal Cemetery of Ur: Patterns in Death," *Cambridge Archaeological Journal*, 2011.

Sir Leonard Woolley, *Ur of the Chaldees: a Record of Seven Years of Excavation* (New York: Penguin Books, 1950).

Shala
Stewart and Janet Farrar, *The Witches' Goddess: The Feminine Principle of Divinity* (Blaine, WA: Phoenix Publishing, 1987).

Jeremy Black and Anthony Green, *Gods, Demons and Symbols of Ancient Mesopotamia* (University of Texas Press, 1992).

Shamhat
Stephanie Dalley, *Myths from Mesopotamia, Creation, the Flood, Gilgamesh and others*, (Oxford University Press, 2000).

Melissa Hope Ditmore, *Encyclopedia of Prostitution and Sex Work, Volume 1*(Westport, CT: Greenwood Publishing Group, 2006).

Sophus Helle, "New Gilgamesh Fragment: Enkidu's Sexual Exploits Doubled" *Ancient History Encyclopedia*, last modified November 28, 2018. www.ancient.eu/article/1286.

Rivkah Harris, *Gender and Aging in Mesopotamia: The Gilgamesh Epic and Other Ancient Literature* (Norman, OK: University of Oklahoma Press), p. 122-123.

Siduri
N. Sanders, *The Epic of Gilgamesh* (London, England: Penguin Books Ltd, 1960).

A.R. George, The Babylonian Gilgamesh Epic: Introduction, Critical Edition and Cuneiform Texts (Oxford, UK: Oxford University Press, 2003).

Tashmetum
Stephen Bertman, *Handbook to Life in Ancient Mesopotamia* (Oxford, UK: Oxford University Press, 2005).

Chapter 18

"Origin of Day Names" *Almanac*, Dublin, NH: Yankee Publishing, Inc., retrieved June 10, 2018, www.almanac.com/content/origin-day-names.

Neale Donald Walsch, *Conversations with God (Book 3)* (Newburyport, MA: Hampton Roads Pub Co Inc., 1998), p. 48.

Stephen Tompkins, "Why is God not Female?" *BBC News*, June 2, 2015, www.bbc.com/news/magazine-32960507.

Notes for the Images

Chapter 1

Edwin J. Prittie, 1913, "The Goddess Ishtar Appears to Sargon, the Gardener's Lad" in the book *The story of the greatest nations*.

Marie-Lan Nguyen, 2009—statue of goddess Narundi in the Louvre Museum, Paris. She's wearing the kaunakes, with Elamite and Akkadian inscriptions. The head of this statue was found on the acropolis at Susa by Jacques de Morgan in 1904 and the body in 1907.

Chapter 2

L. Gruner, 1853—"Chaos Monster and Sun God." Black and white crop of full engraving plate scan from the eight feet by eight inches high limestone discovered in the ruins of Nineveh. The bas-reliefs are in the British Museum. There are at least two interpretations of what the image is/was intended to represent. Some sources interpret it as Marduk fighting Tiamat. Some modern sources state it's probably the Anzu bird and the warrior god Ninurta.

Chapter 3

Cylinder Seal. The variety of mythological scenes increased dramatically during the Akkadian period. In this seal, a seated vegetation goddess, possibly Ninhursag, is greeted by three other deities. Stalks of grain sprout from the females, while tree branches grow from the two males, perhaps referring to a specific myth (circa 2350—2150 BC) It's at the Walters Art Museum in Maryland.

Mesopotamian Goddesses

Chapter 4

Female Head. Ningal UE IV. Marble head of a woman, the eyes inlaid with shell and lapis lazuli. Found near the ruins of a temple built by Dungi. It's currently at Penn Museum.

Chapter 5

The Huluppu-Tree
This image is an accurate, photographic representation of an ancient Akkadian cylindrical seal depicting the goddess Inanna/Ishtar and her sukkal Ninshubur. The seal originates from the Akkad Period and was created sometime circa 2334-2154 BC. It's currently in the Oriental Institute at the University of Chicago.

Inanna and the God of Wisdom
Akkadian cylinder seal from c. 2300 BC or thereabouts depicting the deities Inanna, Utu, Enki, and Isimud. These figures can be identified as gods by their pointed hats with multiple horns. The figure with streams of water and fish flowing from its shoulders is Ea (Sumerian Enki), god of subterranean waters and of wisdom. Behind him stands Usimu, his two-faced vizier (chief minister). At the center of the scene is the sun-god, Shamash (Sumerian Utu), with rays rising from his shoulders. He is cutting his way through the mountains in order to rise at dawn. To his left is a winged goddess, Ishtar (Sumerian Inanna). The weapons rising from her shoulders symbolize her warlike characteristics. This is at the British Museum Collections.

Courtship of Inanna and Dumuzi
A Sumerian plaque depicting the marriage of the goddess Inanna with Sumerian King Dumizi.

Descent of Inanna

This is known as the "Burney Relief" or the "Queen of the Night" which is believed to represent either Ishtar or her older sister Ereshkigal (c. 19th or 18th century BC). It's housed in the British Museum.

Rectangular, baked clay relief panel; modeled in relief on the front depicting a nude female figure with tapering feathered wings and talons, standing with her legs together; shown full frontal, wearing a headdress consisting of four pairs of horns topped by a disc; wearing an elaborate necklace and bracelets on each wrist; holding her hands to the level of her shoulders with a rod and ring in each; figure supported by a pair of adored lions above a scale-pattern representing mountains or hilly ground, and flanked by a pair of standing owls.

Chapter 6

Stele showing Ishtar holding a bow from Ennigaldi-Nanna's Museum (eighth century BC).

Ancient Mesopotamian terracotta relief showing Gilgamesh slaying the Bull of Heaven, sent by Ishtar in Tablet VI of the *Epic of Gilgamesh* after he spurns her amorous advances. The relief is kept at the Royal Museums of Art and History in Brussels.

Lions were one of Inanna-Ishtar's primary symbols. The lion in this image comes from the Ishtar Gate, the eighth gate to the inner city of Babylon, which was constructed in around 575 BC under the orders of Nebuchadnezzar II. This is at the Pergamon Museum in Berlin.

Mesopotamian Goddesses

Chapter 7

Enlil and Ninlil (Sud) on ancient city wall.

Chapter 8

Ancient Sumerian bas-relief portrait depicting Enheduanna (c. 2350-2300 BC).

A ritual scene where a priest makes a libation in front of a four-story altar (left), accompanied by three people, including the priestess Enheduanna in prayer pose (third person coming from the right). The back of the disk bears an inscription, a dedication from Enheduanna to the moon god.

Chapter 9

Impression of a Sumerian cylinder seal from the Early Dynastic III period (ca. 2600 BC; see Woolley 1934, pl. 200, no. 102 [BM 121545]). Persons drinking beer are depicted in the upper row. The habit of drinking beer together from a large vessel using long stalks went out of fashion after the decline of Sumerian culture in the second millennium BC.

The temples issued workers with daily rations of barley beer, the staple drink of Mesopotamia. Late Uruk Period, 3100-3000 BC. The British Museum.

Chapter 10

Kudurru depicting Goddess Gula with her dog, kudurru of

Nazimarutash, from the temple of Marduk, Babylon during the second half of the fourteenth century BCE. This is at the Louvre Museum in France.

Chapter 11

Goddess standing, probably Nanshe. She is accompanied by two geese and holds a vase in her hand. Water and fish emerge from the vase. Two six-pointed starts and two solar disks are behind the goddess. University of Pennsylvania Museum.

Chapter 12—Semiramis

David Castor, 2009, Shamshi-Adad V, Assyrian king 823–811 BC. The pictures shows a stele at the British Museum in London.

Ernest Wallcousins, 1915, *The Shepherd finds the Babe Semiramis*—from *Myths of Babylonia and Assyria* by D. MacKenzie.

Francesco Barbieri, 1624, Semiramis hearing of the insurrection at Babylon. This is at the Museum of Fine Arts in Boston.

Giovanni Francesco Barbieri, 1624, A depiction of the legendary Assyrian queen Semiramis being informed of the Revolt of Babylon in 626 BCE.

Chapter 13

Asherah, detail from an ivory box from Mīnat al-Bayḍā' near Ras Shamra (Ugarit), Syria, c. 1300 BC. This is in the Louvre, Paris.

Mesopotamian Goddesses

Chapter 14

(1) Michelangelo, 1512, *The Fall of Adam and Eve* as depicted in the Sistine Chapel, Vatican.

(2) Gabriel Charles Dante Rossetti, 1866-1868, *Lady Lilith*. This is in the Delaware Art Museum.

Chapter 15

Relief of the goddess Kububa, holding a pomegranate in her right hand and a mirror in her left hand; orthostat relief from Herald's wall, Carchemish ; 850-750 BC; Museum of Anatolian Civilizations, Ankara, Turkey.

Chapter 16

Bas-relief of Nemesis, al-Lat and the dedicator, second or third century CE, at the Museum of Fine Arts of Lyon.

Chapter 17

Reconstructed Sumerian headgear necklaces found in the tomb of Puabi, housed at the British Museum.

Chapter 18

Painting of the Madonna and Child by an anonymous Italian, first half of 19th century.